Starmont Reader's Guide 40

Isaac Asimov

Donald M. Hassler
Series Editor: Roger C. Schlobin

BORGO PRESS / WILDSIDE PRESS

www.wildsidepress.com

Dedication

To Isaac Asimov, for his help with details of fact and for the work itself;
To Roger Schlobin and Ted Dikty, for all the books in this series;
To the English Department and Research Council of Kent State University for continuing help;
To the Science Fiction Foundation of London, England, for permission to reprint portions of chapter five that appeared in *Foundation;*
To my father, Donald M. Hassler, 1905-1985, whose name I sign intentionally as mine.
 —Kent, Ohio

Library of Congress Cataloging-in-Publication Data

Hassler, Donald M.
 Isaac Asimov.

 (Starmont reader's guide ; 40)
 Bibliography: p.
 Includes Index.
  1. Asimov, Isaac, 1920-   --Criticism and interpretation.
 2. Science fiction, American--History and criticism. I. Title. II. Series.
 PS3551.S5Z625   1991   813'.54   86-14585
 ISBN 0-930261-32-1
 ISBN 0-930261-31-3 (pbk.)

copyright © 1991 by Starmont House, Inc.

DONALD M. HASSLER is professor of English at Kent State University in Kent, Ohio. His volume, *Hal Clement,* in this series appeared in June 1982.

Acknowledgments

Chapter 1 was first published in Kent, Ohio by the Kent State University Press, Summer 1987, in *Extrapolation,* volume 28, #2, pps. 187-94. I express my gratitude to Kent State University Press for permission to reprint. Chapter 5 appeared earlier in slightly different form in *Foundation,* #37 (Autumn 1986), pps. 22-30. A portion from Chapter 6 appeared earlier as a review of *Foundation and Earth* in *Fantasy Review,* #98 (Jan/Feb 1987), p. 32. I am grateful to the editors and publishers for permission to reprint.

CONTENTS

	Chronology and Canon	1
I	Science Fiction and High Art	4
II	The Campbell Years and All the Short Stories	18
III	Calvin Robot Books and The Foundation Trilogy	37
IV	Three Early Novels and the Juveniles	56
V	Robot Novels and Two Non-Series Novels	75
VI	Late Novels at the Cutting Edge	96
VII	Conclusion	112
VIII	Selectively Annotated Primary Bibliography	116
IX	Selectively Annotated Secondary Bibliography	122
	Index	126

CHRONOLOGY AND CANON

As he affirms explicitly in his *Autobiography* and implicitly in what he has listed in *Who's Who in America,* Asimov's books constitute a major portion of what has taken place in his life; thus the list of his science-fiction works at the end of this study is also a chronology.

1920   Born January 2 in Petrovichi, Russia, to Judah Asimov and Anna Berman Asimov (the date may have been some months earlier).

1923   Emigrated with family to Brooklyn.

1928   Became naturalized U.S. citizen.

1929   Started reading science-fiction pulps in his father's candy store and added these to his prodigious early reading.

1935   Began Seth Low Junior College; first fan letter in *Astounding;* both his education and fan writing were prodigious.

1936   Began studies at Columbia University.

1938   Started a diary; joined Futurians; began series of visits to John W. Campbell at the offices of *Astounding*.

1939   First published story printed in *Amazing Stories,* and a few months later the July issue of *Astounding* carried his first Campbell story; earned B.S. degree at Columbia.

1940   Continued visits to Campbell and worked on
1941   robot stories, foundation stories, as well as others; wrote "Nightfall"; took M.A. degree at Columbia but failed first time he took qualifying examinations for Ph.D.

1942   Passed second try at Ph.D. tests, but he postponed further graduate work to take a job as chemist at the U.S. Navy Yard in Philadelphia; married Gertrude Blugerman.

1945   Drafted into the Army.

1946   Received a "research discharge" from the Army as a corporal to resume Ph.D. work.

1948   Earned Ph.D. at Columbia.

1949   Joined the faculty of the School of Medicine of Boston University, Biochemistry Department.

1950   First two books published.

1951   Birth of son David; promotion to rank of assistant professor.

1955   Birth of daughter Robyn; promoted to associate professor.

1958   Left full-time teaching for writing but retained his associate professorship; he was publishing more non-fiction.

1963   Awarded a "Special Hugo" at the Worldcon for his non-fiction, science articles in *Fantasy and Science Fiction*.

1965   Received the James T. Grady Award of the American Chemical Society.

1966 Foundation Trilogy awarded the Hugo.

1967 Received the American Association for the Advancement of Science (AAAS) Westinghouse Prize for writing about science.

1969 Published his 100th book.

1970 Moved back to New York from Boston; separated from Gertrude Asimov.

1973 Received both the Nebula and Hugo Awards for *The Gods Themselves;* married to Dr. Janet Jeppson.

1976 Associated with founding of the magazine *Isaac Asimov's Science Fiction Magazine*.

1977 Received both the Nebula and Hugo Awards for "The Bicentennial Man."

1979 Published his 200th book and promoted to full professor.

1983 Received Award of Excellence from Alumni of Columbia University; also Hugo Award for *Foundation's Edge;* underwent triple bypass heart operation.

1984 Published his 300th book.

1986 Published his fifth "Foundation" volume titled *Foundation and Earth* in October.

1987 Awarded the Grand Master Award at Nebula Banquet in May.

I. SCIENCE FICTION AND HIGH ART

Two characteristics seem central to Isaac Asimov's immense writing productivity over nearly fifty years. One is a strong self-confident energy he calls his "rationality"; the other is his almost militant disregard for the decorums and high expectations of artistic literature. Both these are puzzling characteristics to students of literature, who usually expect many more types of ambiguity and who only recently have begun to point out and to praise artistic effects even in science fiction. At the same time, Asimov's unambiguous rationality and his anti-literary stance appeal to some traditionally-trained students.[1] Further, Asimov begins his own massive autobiography by noting that there is less to say about his life than his books (and already we see the paradox of the anti-literary writer as literary theorist) since all he has done is write from a very early age.[2] This opening chapter will introduce not only a bit about his "life" but also what his life as a writer has meant both for the literary community as a whole and for the smaller science-fiction community.

Also, it would be impossible here to write about everything Asimov has produced. His canon ranges from science itself to Biblical commentary to detective fiction. So the advantage in this limitation provides, in another way, the chance to say something about Asimov's science fiction as a key part of modern culture and literature. As I have written elsewhere, one traditional way to read Asimov's fiction is in terms of an ambiguity in tone. Complexity of statement, such as this, would represent the mimetic role of the high artist in which some fundamental truth about existence is sensed by the artist and "imitated" in the mysterious and extra-rational unity of the work of art.[3] Such a traditional rationale for explaining the effect of works of art, in this case fiction, could come into play in examining Asimov's science fiction. However, I have come to think now that the overall "paraliterary" effects in his fiction are more important. Science fiction in this time is not identical in effect, or intention, to the "high art" of recent artistic literary tradition. No author embodies the difference more than Asimov in his energy and his antiliterary views.

Asimov's anti-literary stance seems genuine and interesting—though, of course, it might also be a preemptive defense, such as traditionally quirky poets like Robert Frost have put up against the readings of critics. A key difference remains, however, between the poets who play coy with their critics, who are in many cases their fellow academics, and pulp writers who grew up in the marketplace influenced by editors, such as John W. Campbell who trained as an engineer and was dedicated to the paraliterary effects of a "popular" literature. When I began my study of Hal Clement (Starmont House, 1982), another Campbell writer, Clement's attitude of apparent total unconcern with the expert opinions in the academic literary community struck me as significant. Shortly after my talks with him, which seemed mutually enjoyable, Clement wrote in *Analog* about a question that had come up over the chemistry in his latest novel:

> I am absolutely delighted to have a reviewer criticize a book on scientific grounds . . . ; I was beginning to fear that the English departments had taken over.[4]

Asimov seems to sense himself even more "outside" of the academic literary establishment than Clement, and this is an extremely interesting and significant characteristic. He readily assumes the attitude in print. For example, here is his response when he was asked recently to review some books: "I know nothing about literature. I am not an English major, I never took courses in writing. I have not even thought deeply on the subject. I am just a chemist."[5] Usually Asimov is less brief about the matter. In a fairly long disclaimer, which he wrote as an invited appendage to a collection of critical and scholarly essays about his fiction, he makes use of an image that serves both to separate nicely his thinking from the circuitous and often overtly mysterious effects of high art and to express a key effect of his rationality. His stance against the mystery of high art is consistent with his rationality and a continual theme. In what follows, he is speaking of why he could not be expected to be as literary as his critics; there is the wonderful Swiftian irony of the horse who declares himself a beast to the Yahoos:

> How, then, can I possibly have the time to engage in the kind of deep and intricate thought that would create anything deep and intricate in my stories. . . .My way of working is to. . .take off like a bullet, racing ahead. It is also the only

way of explaining the clarity of my output (and the clearness of my style is remarked on by every reviewer without exception). If I didn't say exactly what I wanted to say as simply as I could say it, I couldn't race ahead as I do.[6]

In fact, not only that collection of critical essays but also this study and the many books on Asimov's work all do say that his work is not straight or simple. But, at the same time, the key fact is that his straightforwardness is his "program." In a world where humanity knows not only that space is curved but also that the human psyche may be equally circuitous (even despairingly circular with the eternal truths of human limitation continually repeating themselves), Asimov's program, and the program of much science fiction, is unashamedly linear. Outwardly, at least, and consistently he has tried in all his work to assume the rational, "Enlightenment" posture of a Voltaire by attacking infamous superstition and promoting progress in a direct manner. Here is what a reviewer writes about one of Asimov's most recent books—an interesting textual document that I will pay more attention to later:

> The most revealing comment by Asimov occurs when he mentions that in his books, both fiction and non-fiction, he tries to "explain the world in a natural, rationalist way, with the confident certainty that one has but to do that to cause people to abandon their foolish superstitions." . . .[this] is a profound expression of the worldview of a rational secular humanist.[7]

Asimov's debt to the 18th-century Enlightenment, however, both in his lifestyle and in his texts, goes beyond his attacks on superstition and his hope for rationality and for progress. It has to do with his basic methodology and, in particular, with the relation between his stance against high art and his rationality. Reason, in this case, is less a distinct faculty of the mind, as it had been for John Milton, than an "open" method for liberating thought and even for speeding up the process of getting results—"racing ahead."[8] This emphasis on open-ended methodology brings into question and, in fact, is a competing methodology against expert opinion, specialist work, and any sort of mysterious or "special" procedure. The instinctive move against the special and the expert is, at the same time, the reliance upon the most sensible rationality.

So Asimov speaks out against the special "priesthood' of literature (or any cultural priesthood) and for a methodology open to anyone, and he invites a "popular" literature in this sense of open-ended rationality., The sense of community in science-fiction fandom has always been strong and attractive; I remember hearing Asimov with tears in my eyes when he gave his short acceptance speech of the 1983 Hugo Award for *Foundation's Edge* and said that he was accepting for all fans at the World Science Fiction Convention. His ego is tempered by his feeling of human community, and the two are not inconsistent since the rationality that drives his ego is a move toward shared knowlege. Most top scientific investigators are gifted and driven thinkers (often with large egos), but their Enlightenment methodology is necessarily open to all investigators—and most effective for this reason.

All the anecdotal evidence in places such as Damon Knight's history of the "Futurians," which gives views of the early Asimov that will be glossed by Asimov himself in the discussion of his early stories in the next chapter, suggests a self-assertive aggressiveness in Asimov that was fully developed at an early age. But the monumental autobiographical urges in this highly prolific writer date from anthologies he began to edit in the early sixties and, of course, have not slacked off since then.[9] Again, the best paradigm for understanding this sort of tactic and its relations both to rationality and to literature may come from 18th-century Enlightenment thinkers. Even more than his highly individualistic colleagues, such as Diderot or La Mettrie, for instance, Jean-Jacques Rousseau is the "Age of Reason" spokesman who teaches most clearly that clear investigation of the way things are must be associated with a strong, assertive, first-person speaker.

From Rousseau, the thread of theoretic development that leads ultimately to the modern para-literature of science fiction passes next through the struggles among the British Romantics over the relevance and reality of literature. The effect in high art to which much science fiction is most opposed are the mimetic mysteries of revelation or intuition. The British Romantics themselves, though they are now central to the tradition called high art, were trying to rethink just these mysteries in an "Enlightenment" manner. (No doubt the stance of the outsiders of science fiction at some time in the future will also be accepted into the tradition.) Most important here, though, is a distinction Samuel Taylor Coleridge felt had to be made between fancy and imagination. This distinction helps to make it clear that Asimov's straightline rationality has, in fact, a long ancestry of being "imaginative."

According to Coleridge, the fully integrated first-person, or "ego," of the imagination, as he has learned it from Rousseau, is both the truest scientific investigator and the best author; they are intellects able to construct images more authentic than the illusions of the fancy.[10] In short, the literature of "fancy" is an entirely different breed of writing from Asimov's. Moreover, the indeterminacies and unconscious uncertainties inside this Coleridgean ego of "imagination" are simply more evidence of its importance in any rational and non-illusioned search. In recent times, Sigmund Freud has confirmed Coleridge's emphasis on imagination over fancy, so it is not surprising that some recent studies of Asimov have begun to uncover layers in his assertive ego that seem distinctly Freudian.[11] Thus the important link is that between ego and rationality. For the purposes of this study of fiction, the rhetoric of ego or "persona" is more to the point than any pathology, or excess, of ego. Also, not just this introductory chapter but the entire discussion that follows will be soaked with Asimov biography. Like the Romantics, he is always in persona.

Another result of this rhetoric of ego is how difficult it is to stay ahead of Asimov's own commentary on his own writing. He continually writes about himself and his own writing. One example is *Asimov on Science Fiction,* which he published in 1981 and since has listed as his 227th book in his *Opus 300*. It will undoubtedly have a sequel soon, since his monthly columns in the magazine with his name in the title are usually about science-fiction writing and his writing.[12] The column in the March 1986, issue is titled "Persona" and confirms, characteristically, the ego not only as a prime tool of his rationality but also as a key tactic in his anti-literary stance. The column begins with Asimov's usual clear assertion that, even though some may accuse him of fabricating a "persona," the speaker of the Good Doctor, who is also the writer delighted with writing and the lover of women, is, in fact, the real Asimov.[13] Whenever he speaks in this first-person assertive way disclaiming all feigning artifice, Asimov reminds me of another Romantic speaker who was also a child of the Enlightenment making good use of the Rousseauistic methodology of the ego, Lord Byron in *Don Juan:*

> There's only one slight difference between Me and my epic brethren gone before . . . They so embellish, that 't is quite a bore Their labyrinth of fables to thread through, Whereas this story's actually true.[14]

Whether or not it is true of Byron, although the encyclopedic text of his poem is clearly suggestive of it, Asimov moves back and forth from ego to the more extended ego of his science-fiction community (Byron had his own rebel-poet community). In other words, the reality of an everyday sense of community is as important as that of ego; both are hard, analyzable contexts rather than the illusions of fancy. In the short persona column, Asimov quickly moves from the opening refutation of the notion of "persona" to a defense of his reputation as a flirtatious gallant. He does this by introducing an unsigned letter apparently from Arthur C. Clarke that makes light of the fame of "the Good Doctor...[as] one of the world's great lovers."¹⁵ The reader suspects that Asimov has made up the letter (he has a letter from Clarke, in fact) which would demonstrate the easy extension of ego into fiction as in many of his stories. Further, some of the arguments in the letter suggest what is really on Asimov's mind. The correspondent points out that the Good Doctor might be distracted from amorous applications by a number of possibilities, the final two of which are that he might get an idea for a short story or Carl Sagan might phone.

This most recent small piece of first-person writing supports a major fact in Asimov's life and in his writing, mentioned already but that needs emphasis to conclude this introductory chapter on the relation of his life to his writing. The fact is the extension of ego into the small community of people that work with science fiction. "Intertextuality" is no doubt the most current literary term for this extension of ego in Asimov. Moreover, the notion of intertextuality can be especially well understood in a study of science fiction since, long before the use of this term became fashionable, science-fiction writers "mingled" texts and worked almost as small tribal communities on a literature they, at least, thought was new. Just as Asimov's ego may beckon the psychoanalytic critics, so the sense of community so strong in the genre invites extensive theory.¹⁶ Again, Asimov anticipates critical theory on this matter of intertextuality. The first fiction of his examined in the next chapter (from *The Early Asimov*) is work that he himself has put into the context of the genre as a whole, and his 1974 anthology *Before the Golden Age* is particularly significant as his expression of the web of intertextuality.¹⁷ In fact, this extreme self-consciousness among the genre writers themselves about how they worked as a community, which Asimov has picked up as a major theme in his numerous retrospective anthologies, has been so apparent from the start that critics and scholars have come to ignore the obvious as mere "fannish" enthusiasm. One book-length study recently devoted to this topic of the "formulas" in the early years states the intertextual self-consciousness clearly: ". . .this formula methodology implies that future work in the field would do well to look more closely at the underlying similarities and not so much at the surface variety of [science fiction]."[18]

Again, Asimov's lengthy autobiography, which ought to be due also for a sequel soon, is the map that best shows this web of intertextuality, or of extended ego, which, along with the drive to rationality examined in detail in the chapters that follow, represent the foundation for his anti-literary confidence. One typical passage is the "entry" for the 21st of January, 1957, that, according to the methodology he outlines in the text itself, was originally an entry in the diary that Asimov has kept since 1938 and recast into its proper position in volume two of the autobiography:

> My eighth teaching semester began on January 21, 1957, and three days later I received a copy of the March 1939 *Amazing* from Forrie Ackerman. It was the one that contained my first story, "Marooned off Vesta." It was eighteen years since that magazine had first appeared, alive, on the stands. I had been a professional writer, now, for nearly half my life.[19]

Asimov continually keeps track of where he is in his life, and this location is surrounded by the usual running discussion of his work and his work with the editors of the pulp magazines: H.L. Gold, Fred Pohl, and always Campbell. Thus for Asimov (as it seems for so many other writers of his generation in the genre), more than any family, social, or religious context, the context of the science-fiction world itself made up the most vital context—an intertext. This relationship was not only one of themes but more importantly one of methodology that also seems to extend backward to the *philosophes* of the 18th-century Enlightenment.

As one final introductory illustration of the major unifying characteristics that make Asimov's fiction important and so "alien," in a sense, from high art, I will extend this web of intertextuality farther forward and farther backward from the central core of modern science fiction in the community of Pohl, Campbell, and Clarke. Carl Sagan's first novel, *Contact*, appeared just as I thought I was completing my research for this book. (This is a vain impossibility, of course, as Asimov writes faster than most of us can read.) So as I read Sagan casually for recreation, the dynamic of "intertextual" science fiction began to take over. I was noticing echoes of Asimov, of Pohl, of James Gunn, of Stanislaw Lem. When I checked Asimov's autobiography, I found the following recollection of his first meeting with this writer, who as the column from the March 1986, *Isaac Asimov's Science Fiction Magazine* (IASFM) indicates, now has the interest to distract the Good Doctor even from the fairer sex:

> On that birthday [Asimov's daughter's 8th, on

February 19, 1963], I met astronomer Carl Sagan, then of Harvard, and had lunch with him. We had already corresponded and I had received some of his papers. He was an ardent science-fiction reader. . . . I had to add him to Marvin Minsky [the computer and artificial intelligence expert] and thereafter I would say that there were two people whom I would readily admit were more intelligent than I was. We have been very good friends ever since.[20]

This network of friendship, the web of context and eventual intertextuality, depends clearly in this case upon intelligence and rationality. Moreover, Sagan himself extends the web backward in time in a particularly suggestive manner with his choice of an illustration for the first edition of his novel. He writes about his choice:

> . . .a high form of intelligence might live at the center of the Milky Way Galaxy. The idea has antecedents, as all ideas do, and something similar seems to have been envisioned around 1750 by Thomas Wright, the first person to mention explicitly that the Galaxy might have a center. A woodcut by Wright depicting the center of the Galaxy is shown on the title page [of Sagan's novel].[21]

Most of the ideas of Thomas Wright, the landscape architect and sometime astronomer from the middle of the 18th century, have faded into the pages of scholarship whereas both Sagan and Asimov are at full brilliance as popular writing stars. But the network is the same, and it is a network of Enlightenment illumination and rationality rather than the arcane mysteries of high art. Asimov's fictions examined in the following chapters suggest the nature of this rationality, the importance of the Enlightenment network, and thus one essential difference of science fiction from other literature.

NOTES

>Some notes concluding this introductory chapter in particular cite theoretic discussions of the nature of science fiction, paraliterature, deconstruction, psychoanalytic criticism, and related topics. Although the scope of this Starmont series precludes extensive treatment of these topics, I am convinced of their importance to Asimov's work and want to recommend them to readers in this way.

1. A recent and typical example of the argument that disparages Asimov's work as not literary enough can be found in the otherwise fine study of Kim Stanley Robinson, *The Novels of Philip K. Dick* (Ann Arbor: UMI Research Press, 1984).
2. Isaac Asimov, *In Memory Yet Green: The Autobiography of Isaac Asimov 1920-1954* (New York: Doubleday, 1979): ix.
3. My own earlier work on Asimov as well as a discussion of the growing theoretic literature that attempts to describe science fiction in general is best seen in my *Comic Tones in Science Fiction* (Westport, CT: Greenwood, 1982). More recently, I am particularly indebted to ideas about "paraliterature" as it differs from the "tradition" in Christopher Pawling, ed., *Popular Fiction and Social Change* (New York: St. Martin's, 1984).
4. Hal Clement, letter, *Analog*, December 1981: 173. For further theoretic ideas about hard science fiction, see also my *Reader's Guide to Hal Clement* (Mercer Island, WA: Starmont, 1982).
5. Asimov, letter, *Fantasy Review*, December 1985: 40.

6. Asimov, "Asimov's Guide to Asimov," *Isaac Asimov,* Writers of the 21st Century Series, ed. Joseph D. Olander and Martin Harry Greenberg (New York: Taplinger, 1977): 202.
7. Elton T. Elliott, "Raising Hackles," rev. of *The Alternate Asimovs* by Isaac Asimov, *Science Fiction Review,* Spring 1986: 53.

II. THE CAMPBELL YEARS & ALL THE SHORT STORIES

Many critics writing on Asimov's fiction have argued that the shorter forms not only are where he began but also constitute his extent of narrative competence. Still others argue that science fiction itself is best seen as a short story genre.[1] Asimov's mind set from the start, however, tended toward large general themes and hence toward longer and longer narratives. For example, his very short story "Black Friar of the Flame," examined in more detail later in this chapter, is his first attempt at future history and at large social questions; thus, it is intended to be a longish story. Further, all during his early writing career when he was still at Columbia and during his long conversations with John W. Campbell, Jr., the topics and the themes of his writing are efforts at rational generalizations and at formulating and dramatizing large, important ideas. Asimov's detractors say that these are mediocre and commonplace ideas.[2] Thus, my purpose in this chapter will be twofold: to describe Asimov's start as a fiction writer and his early associations with Campbell and Frederik Pohl and to assess the importance of his short fiction. This assessment will concern both the early stories that anticipate large ideas, which eventually find better expression in longer sets of narrative, and the later stories that stand on their own but that are not as effective as the novels and series.

Also, this chapter and following chapters each will be primarily organized around a form or a text, such as short story, series, novel, juvenile. These parallel Asimov's writing career and provide somewhat of a chronological approach as well. In addition to working with one or another form and throughout his chronological development, Asimov's intention and motivation simply to write must be noticed. A statement by Asimov himself on his earliest intentions in writing is an appropriate place to start:

> ...one of my products was accepted for the semiannual literary magazine [at Boys' High in 1934] while many [of those of the other boys] were rejected. Unfortunately the teacher told me, with callous insensitivity, that mine was the only item submitted that was humorous and that since he had to have *one* non-tragic piece he was forced to take it....I wonder what happened to all those great tragic writers in the class.[3]

He records this self-satisfied opinion almost forty years later as part of his ongoing autobiographical interpretation of his own work; and before interpreting it myself, I want to cite another typical Asimovian boast that is thrown off in some introductory paragraphs written within a year or so of the introductions to *The Early Asimov*, that is, decades after the start of his writing career: "Yesterday, someone said to me that a critic was like a eunuch in a harem. He could observe, study, and analyze—but he couldn't do it himself."[4]

As I suggested in the opening chapter, then, Asimov is a writer driven by parallel compulsions. He must always prove he is potent as a writer; as a boy of fourteen even, the stakes seemed so high to him that he must not risk losing. This energy and resilience, which seems at the same time both boastful and careful, marks all his writing tactics from early youth on. Clearly, this is insecurity, but in another sense it is a program of trying again and again and of gradually accumulating competence. One of the strongest examples of this method of building from weakness is in Enlightenment thinking. A person might be a stubborn and "tragic" martyr for revealed truth or religion, but the process, and insecurity, of continually accumulating more information towards the infinitely illusive truths of nature represents a "comic" resilience that can be found in Asimov's life and fiction. As a methodology, this program stems from the Enlightenment, and as I suggested in the opening chapter, it makes good use of the insecurities and quirks of personality.

He was, of course, fortunate—in the early years of his writing— to find another "Enlightenment" rationalist, John Campbell, to both sell stories to and talk with. The first sale he made to Campbell, the story titled "Trends," is a clear harbinger of all Asimov's thought and of much Campbellian hard science fiction. The inventor in the story who has an attitude of gradualism and comic patience that allows him to wait out failure and to learn by mistakes, which is exactly the methodological program of the young Asimov learning gradually to produce stories that will sell, actually invokes the Enlightenment. In the quotation that follows, the "momentary reaction" that Asimov has his inventor-hero character mention represents the unenlightened fanaticism of religion; his own instincts, and Campbell's coaching favored reason:

> We're going through a momentary reaction following a period of too-rapid advance in the Mad Decades [according to the fictional history of the story these would have been the decades of Einstein, Bohr, and the new physics]. Just

such a reaction took place in the Romantic Age—the first Victorian Period—following the too-rapid advance of the eighteenth-century Age of Reason.[5]

It is in presenting this first *Astounding* sale, also (in *The Early Asimov* more than thirty years later), that the question of literary models and influences comes up. Asimov acknowledges what by then was very apparent in his writing. He recollects that he had named the narrator in "Trends" after Clifford Simak because he, and other Campbell writers, had learned how to construct stories from the pulp masters of the 1930s, such as Simak. Moreover, he notes that by the time he was beginning to sell stories it was a shibboleth that a science-fiction writer not even try to imitate James Joyce.[6] Seen from another perspective, here is what the British "New Wave" leader, J.G. Ballard, says about the group of writers that Campbell was assembling that included Asimov, Pohl, Sturgeon, Heinlein, and many others:

> . . .they would move around the States like something out of *On the Road,* living together in litle groups and enclaves. There were all of these collaborations going on, and they just surfaced now and again at an SF convention, and plunged around in endless car-rides—a strange sort of Bonny-and Clyde existence. They never seemed to meet anyone outside that little world.[7]

Ballard's choice of imagery actually makes them seem more "literary" than he probably intended by invoking the Beat poets, and Asimov himself never has liked to travel—Jack Williamson and Edmund Hamilton fit the car-riding image more. Asimov, however, did "travel" from Boooklyn to pay visits to Campbell's office just at the time he began writing his early stories and paid nearly monthly visits to this Manhattan office until his move to Philadelphia during the war. Even then, Asimov would return to see Campbell on the weekends. The influence that Ballard suggests was strong. It was not until the end of the decade, when Asimov took his faculty position in Boston, that the direct effect of Campbell's continual conversation and flow of ideas became more removed. Asimov and many others of this group have written often about the nature and impact of Campbell's ideas on science fiction.[8] Campbell's letters also attest to the energy and programmatic thrust of his editorial work. Here is Campbell writing about a program of gradual "Enlightenment" to Poul Anderson in 1952:

> Science-fiction is far more advanced in understanding than the general culture. . . . We are [he mentions Asimov in a list of writers in the line above], in essence, trying to teach the most thoughtful, speculative and philosophical group of Mankind. . .a quite new viewpoint. It isn't something they know they want to learn; therefore we have to do it by entertaining them enough so that they'll accept the new ideas for the *sake of entertainment,* rather than for the *sake of the idea.* [In other words, a didactic rather than mimetic literature.][9]

Up until the time that he left New York City for Boston and his first book was about to appear *(Pebble in the Sky),* Asimov wrote about sixty stories, including all the Foundation and most of the positronic robot series. Though some of his best short stories come later (and the several long series will be discussed here in later chapters), these Campbell-influenced stories that begin his career are exciting reading. Many of them, as one would expect, contain the effects of large generalization that are so important to the understanding of Asimov's fiction. None of these ideas that Asimov and Campbell share at this time may be seen as strictly scientific; however, they are all rational in the sense of being general, non-mysterious, and consistent. One notorious blind spot or bias Campbell alone possessed was his notion of the superiority, at least specialness, of human beings and especially of Anglo-Saxon Americans.[10] Other than this prejudice, which Asimov himself may have been overly sensitive to in his own extreme liberalness of temper, Campbell was a man of the Enlightenment whose ideas eventually led to Asimov's own theory of social science fiction and whose vision shaped the young writer into a rational extrapolator.

The basic pattern of this large, general vision borrowed from the 18th-century Enlightenment thinkers and seasoned with the popular success of modern science and technology was one of gradual accumulation of knowledge and eventual rational control as opposed to fanaticism, superstition, or parochial, local power. Asimov stretches this pattern of "clear reason" far into the past and far to the future to create the embryonic images for what he calls "psychohistory." It works for rationally consistent, human civilizations that extend across interstellar distances and especially for the rise and fall of Golden Ages. The continuing epic battle between reason and unreason will recur again and again as a theme in his fiction. Moreover, this vision of control and of generality is always governed by Asimov's understanding of human history. It is as though he must always anchor his imagination in realities, such as recorded history and current science; sheer fancy plays little part in this fiction. Also, there is continually a tension between open-ended analysis that is the driving force behind change and large general movement, on the one hand, and just coping as humans on the others. Perhaps one reason some critics dismiss Asimov's fiction, along with much science fiction, as less than artistic is that he is seldom satisfied to depict human character. He seems always to want to work toward large, general human interpretations, such as psychohistory or insights into the ebb and flow of history—Galactic Empires, lost Golden Ages. This is true in his early stories, but now and then he hints at what he is giving up by pursuing the big ideas. In the sequel to "Homo Sol," his first Galactic Empire story that also includes a psychologist who works in the direction of Hari Seldon's big breakthrough, the rational planner pauses from his work for a moment, but this is the exception because it is rare in these early stories for a character to set aside hard work and large ideas:

> Words, phrases, equations spun through his keen brain, but he was happy in spite of them. And in a little while, the human triumphed over the psychologist and Porus abandoned analysis for the superior joy of uncritical happiness.[11]

Asimov's vision from the Campbell years is characterized, then, by its pursuit of the general rather than the individual so that the role of humans is always in question. His robots, examined in the next chapter, provide some interesting answers to this problematic question of "the human," anticipated even in stories that are not strictly robot stories from these early years. Here is what an early character says about some robotic humanoids who are New Yorkers and, actually, very much like Asimov himself: ". . .they *must* have perseverance which practically implies stubbornness and combativeness."[12] Asimov's own ability to persevere along with his combative ego were just getting started in these early years.

As the decade of the 1950s began and Asimov had a fulltime teaching job at Boston University, he continued to produce short fiction, though longer pieces were becoming more important for the ideas he wanted to express in fiction. By the end of the decade, he was committed to turning out much more non-fiction than any sort of fiction. He published three book-length collections of his short fiction between 1955 and 1959, and perhaps his most well-constructed short stories date from this period. I will save for the end of this chapter discussion of his most well-known short story, "Nightfall," which he had written much earlier for Campbell, and add a discussion of a very typical interchange between him and Campbell over the ending of an important story, "Belief." Asimov himself has documented that Campbell revision for his critics and interpreted it as he has been so wont to do in his later career. Once again, this seems to be a case of the anti-literary writer who wants to be his own interpretor, his own generalist. Asimov may not be the most reliable commentator on his own work and often does not even mention some of the most important parallels and themes, as a closer examination will show, that give his work meaning.

For example, he comments in a later collection of the "Best of Asimov" stories that the 1952 story "The Martian Way" was intended to criticize the political abuses of the McCarthy era as a sort of satire.[13] However, most readers will notice the narrowness and infamous machinations of politicians on Earth seem less important as images in the narrative than do the radical notions about human character and about the general outward expansion of humanity. Humans living on Mars are different in nature, and though literature itself is not mentioned, presumbably a wider human perspective will call for different sorts of stories, for a different literature. The main character, Ted Long, actually has much in common with the space ranger, David Starr, about whom Asimov was centering his series of juvenile novels at this same time. Both are orphans of pioneer astronauts who died in space. A part of Asimov always wants to cut ties with earth or with earthbound humanity. Further, this is not a negative movement in "The Martian Way," but rather the positive corollary of the general movement outward to Galactic Empire. The problem that Long and his fellow Martians solve, however, is in the primitive early stages of space colonization, far earlier than the technological advances that underlie Asimov's galaxy-wide settings. Thus he can write with accuracy and detail about the extrapolated engineering, and along with the space engineering, the reader can sense extrapolation about human character and about literature. People will be different in the progressive future. Here, in fact, can be found eloquent expression of the "Asimov Way" as Long envisions progress:

There'll be starships someday; great, huge things that can carry thousands of people and maintain their self-contained equilibrium for decades, maybe centuries. Mankind will spread through the whole Galaxy. But people will have to live their lives out on ship. . .so it will be Martians, not planet-bound Earthmen, who will colonise the universe. That's inevitable. It's got to be. It's the Martian Way.[14]

At the conclusion to this story, one character is said to be "feeling the future rushing in." Asimov has written a fine phrase and image for the rush of progress thas has been felt off and on by believers in the Enlightenment since those early progressive thinkers argued how possible such change might be.[15] A corollary to that enthusiasm was the fear of the infamous superstition of religion that Voltaire had resolved to wipe out wherever it might be found. This is the anti-religion theme from that early story "Trends" that Campbell had picked up on so quickly and that has stayed with the Asimov/Campbell brand of hard science fiction all the way to the most recent expression of it, such as in Carl Sagan's 1985 novel *Contact* in which religious fanatics are villains.

Even though religious fanatics with a myopic insistence on "eternal values" (this is related, of course, to what the poets and theorists of high art invoke as the "eternal" meaningfulness of literature) keep coming back as the enemy in a fiction as rooted in the Enlightenment, as I believe Asimov's is, the far end of all colonization, the most general idea, must be finally a religious end or idea. Enlightenment beliefs in progressive change, in fact, echo Biblical notions about creation and change in their sublime largeness. In this way, even Voltaire always remained a good Christian. Asimov's Jewish roots and awe of the God of the Hebrews are made manifest in a story from this period, the one that he has said is his favorite.[16] In terms of characterization and largeness of theme, "The Last Question" is indeed consistent with Asimov effects. Ordinary human character is quickly left behind; controls and psychological understanding rapidly become most general; and the big question of all imperial expansion dominates a text that concludes with Biblical echoes. If "The Martian Way" sounds like Carl Sagan, Asimov's "The Last Question" rings echoes of Olaf Stapledon. The true Enlightenment rationalist does not hesitate to incorporate scripture into the text if the generalizing theme has moved to the beginnings: "And it came to pass. . . . The consciousness of AC [analog computer—note in the early days how "analog," not "digital," seemed to be the direction of computing] encompassed all of what had once been a Universe and brooded over. . . ."[17]

Moreover, a very recent short story carries the title "The Last Answer" and suggests the continuing interest over his whole career in the large, general idea that paradoxically, or consistently, points the Enlightenment rationalist firmly in the direction of the Biblical religious tradition. Also appropriate is that this story was written for and first published in the 50th anniversary issue of *Astounding,* and Asimov's comment in the book appearance of the story does speculate about what his great mentor's reaction might have been to his clear extrapolaton on an idea here. This idea, which would have interested Campbell, is the old challenge of Milton's Satan, the cantankerous mental urge to question *whatever* might be the cosmic setup. And just as verbal echoes of the Bible and of Milton occur in "The Last Question," so in "The Last Answer" the reader responds not to character but to large, sublime idea worded to reecho the tradition. Here is the Satan of the story speaking and then "God's" answer:

> "I do not want to think forever to amuse you. I do not want to exist forever to amuse you. All my thinking will be directed toward ending the nexus. *That* would amuse *me*. . . ." "There is not one of those I [God] have with me in this existence of perfect and eternal thought that does not have the ambition of destroying me. It cannot be done."[18]

Thus the Asimov Way is to focus on the general idea. As in much science fiction, the large idea sometimes strikes close to home. Though science fiction is not prediction (rather it seems more like Old Testament prophecy), now and then what is said about the near future in a story does come true. In his most recent collection of his own science-fiction short fiction, *The Winds of Change and Other Stories* (1983), which is his eighth collection of science-fiction short stories (not counting the robot or detective stories), "The Last Shuttle" focuses on the movement of the human race outward, leaving an Earth totally uninhabited by humans as a "monument to humanity's origin." Asimov continually works over this image of the planet of origin in a vastly peopled universe in his major long fictions; it seems to be one of his favorite Golden Age images. What is uncanny here are several sentences in this story that ring painfully true in early 1986:

> [the pilot, a woman, says] "It seems to me that it would be dramatic irony . . . if this last shuttle blew up on takeoff." [her superior answers] "Shuttle lift-offs are trouble free [but recalling the tragedy mentioned in the fiction of 'Enterprise Sixty']. . . . That was a hundred seventy years ago and there has not been a space-related casualty since."[19]

Asimov says he wrote the story in honor of the First Shuttle flight in April 1981; then, in January of 1986, a nation watched on national television as he, with Sagan and others, encouraged continued work for gradual progress, rather than despair, following the *Challenger* tragedy. Now against the tragic events of 1986 and his comments about them, Asimov's most recent short fiction seems to want to escape to the joking tone of 1934. Perhaps it is his comic response to the seriousness of having a magazine that carries his name. The ghost of Campbell haunts many of the editorials he writes for this magazine, which has come to be called simply *Asimov's*, and yet his own story in the celebrating 100th issue is part of a series of "light fantastic" stories beginning early in 1982, which he says he would like eventually to publish in a collection. The "Azazel" stories have, in fact, been made technically into science fiction with a bow to the Arthur C. Clarke dictum on advanced technology: "Azazel is the two-centimeter extraterrestrial that is so advanced. . .that its technological power seems almost magical to ordinary Earth-people"[20] Further, Asimov seems to be using this light fantastic format for some subtle character suggestion. Nevertheless, the dominant effect in this more recent short fiction is the joking tone and, more important, the joking about writing itself. As with his autobiographical outpourings and with his continual commentary over his own work, even Asimov's short fiction lately seems to turn back so self-consciously to his most early adolescent motivations about writing and to his insecurity. Perhaps this recent light tone is some help in keeping him going with large ideas and the gradual accumulation of more work; his recent long fiction, examined in later chapters, is some of his most ambitious. One of his characters, a would-be writer, who will be a recipient of Azazel intervention, writes:

> "It is a matter of little moment to me whether I make money or not, so that I gain immortality and bestow a priceless gift of insight and understanding to all future generations."[21]

Unlike his character, whose existence in the vast collection of Asimovian short fiction represents a sort of hedge or safety-valve, Asimov himself need never joke about nor doubt the seriousness and the successful effects of his best short fiction. In fact, his most recent self-commentary suggests that he does not—so the joking over his desire to be a greater writer is just the counterweight to what he knows is the fact and to what, with his lucid rationality, he will continue to point out and describe. A recent collection of his fiction, published in early 1986, presents a set of variant texts on earlier published stories along with his critical comment. In addition to the commercial motivation, the purpose of *The Alternate Asimovs* is to help map and appreciate his "universe" of rationality and literary seriousness as he intends it to be perceived. One of the most successful inclusions toward this end is the unpublished version of Asimov's 1953 story, written for Campbell, entitled "Belief." In this instance, Campbell had been less rational than Asimov and had insisted on a more upbeat ending to a story that really sets forth most clearly Asimov's Enlightenment methodology of attacking superstition wherever it is found. The one word title that remains unchanged in both versions is ideal for the story, and Asimov's commentary leaves joking aside to pinpoint exactly what is at stake:

> My thesis (not directly expressed. . .but implied over and over) was: "For belief to exist, truth alone is insufficient. . . ." I continue to write books on science and history, and science fiction too, in which I try to explain the world in a natural, rationalist way, with the confident certainty that one has but to do that to cause people to abandon their foolish superstitions.[22]

Such a Voltaire-like program, perhaps because it is always reaching out toward the most general concepts, also serves to represent large and sublime ideas that, though they are not superstitions and are grounded on clear reasoning, are awe inspiring. Asimov's most famous story, "Nightfall," can serve well to illustrate this sense of awe. It is serious and effective in this sublime way that harks back to the Enlightenment methodologies of seeing more clearly and also because it brings into focus many of the characteristics already noted in these short stories and that will figure in later chapters. "Nightfall" is a Campbell story, and the often repeated anecdote about how Asimov was sent home armed with the quotation from Emerson and instructed to make a story is doubly interesting now because Asimov has published in his editorial to the April 1986 issue of *Asimov's* some new information about Campbell's knowledge of the idea. It is highly probable that Campbell had read, in a 1937 issue of *Sky*, a non-fiction piece that had set up and actually worked out in detail a similar situation. Asimov speculates that Campbell had just been waiting to set one of his young writers to work on the images.[23] Paradoxically, Asimov claims "Nightfall" to be his most original story; he himself had no knowledge, in March 1941, of the *Sky* article.

The story is, indeed, powerful and saturated with concepts and images that were passionately interesting to Asimov at the time and that will work through much of his other fiction. The scientists and historians on the planet Lagash are aware of immense cycles of civilization, Golden Age before Golden Age. Religion, or rather a kind of cultism, is simultaneously a harbinger of scientific discovery and a result of the facts of the physical environment. What the characters are most interested in—the discovery of large general truths and psychological as well as physical laws in nature—is exactly what drives them insane. In fact, the real madness that infects Lagash, and which has infected it age after age, is not from the darkness that comes once every two millenia but from the stars. In other words, the disorientation and nausea, as well as the ignorance, that comes with the darkness or the lack of "Enlightenment" is not the major problem. In the story, people go into caves, experience total darkness, and adjust to it. Moreover, scientific ignorance, for people on Lagash as elsewhere, does not cause madness because people can adjust to their ignorance. What destroys the psychologist in the story, as well as the journalist and all the other scientists, is the realization of the vastness of the universe rather than ignorance of that fact. More conditioning, preparation, or education are needed than any civilization on Lagash can muster to face the full Enlightenment of the vastness of the universe as it is revealed each cycle. Long before total eclipse, when all the stars appear, the journalist seems confident that his writing can confront the most immense facts:

> "What an idea for a good Sunday supplement article. Two dozen suns in a universe eight light years across. Wow! That would shrink our world into insignificance. The readers would eat it up."[24]

When the incredibly expanded reality is revealed and the journalist goes mad along with everyone on Lagash, Asimov is suggesting that science fiction itself may possibly be capable of preparing readers more fully for such startling Enlightenment. In any case, the story is a fine accomplishment for a young writer and one that will confirm him in his rational interest in generality. After all, Campbell paid him a bonus for good work.

NOTES

1. The best comprehensive study of Asimov's science fiction to date and one that has been very useful in my preparation for this study is James Gunn's *Isaac Asimov: The Foundations of Science Fiction* (New York: Oxford UP, 1982). Although Gunn admires the longer narratives, he does make the argument strongly here and elsewhere that shorter forms are most characteristic of science fiction. Also Gunn speaks valuably about Asimov's "rationality" but without the emphasis on his move to the "general" and his debt to the Enlightenment.

2. The most scathing recent attack on science fiction in general, with particular reference to Asimov, is Luc Sante, "The Temple of Boredom," *Harper's,* October 1985: 66-71. The accusations of commonplace ideas and non-literary writing in this piece need refuting and have motivated much of my own writing here.
3. Isaac Asimov, *The Early Asimov. Book One* (New York: Ballantine, 1986): 9. *The Early Asimov* was first published by Doubleday in 1972.
4. Asimov, *The Best of Isaac Asimov* (Greenwich: Fawcett, 1976): 12. *The Best of Isaac Asimov* was first published by Doubleday in 1973.
5. Asimov, "Trends," *The Early Asimov, Book One:* 85.
6. The narrator's name is Cliff McKenny, and Asimov says in his comment printed with the story that he chose the name to honor Simak.
7. J.G. Ballard, *J.G. Ballard: The First Twenty Years,* ed. James Goddard and David Pringle (Hayes, Middlesex: Bran's Head, 1976): 14. I am indebted to another volume in this Starmont series for bringing Ballard's views on the American pulp writrers to my attention; Peter Brigg has written the Starmont *J.G. Ballard.*
8. James Gunn's accounts of his interviewing of Asimov are probably the most reliable evidences although Asimov speaks about Campbell in his continual autobiographical writings often. My own work has not included a further interview with Asimov since Gunn has seemed to have done it so well and since Asimov has put so much about himself in print. In any case, I can adopt a certain view of the man in his writing that would not be the same if I were closer to the man in person. Also to the point here is the awe I hold toward the man in person as I allude to in chapter one above in mentioning his acceptance of the Hugo in 1983.
9. John W. Campbell, *The John W. Campbell Letters,* ed. Perry A. Chapdelaine, Sr., Tony Chapdelaine, and George Hay (Franklin, TN: AC Projects, 1985): I, 84. To Poul Anderson, October 25, 1952.
10. In his running commentary throughout *The Early Asimov,* the delicate lines beween Asimov's growing sensitivity to Jewish persecution in Europe and his respect for his wonderful mentor

are clearly sketched. A careful study of all the autobiographical texts on this matter would be important for an understanding of both Asimov and his teacher—but beyond the scope of this book.
11. Asimov, "The Imaginary," *The Early Asimov, Book One:* 250.
12. Asimov, "Death Sentence," *The Early Asimov, Book Two:* 170.
13. Asimov, *The Best of Isaac Asimov:* 11.
14. Asimov, "The Martian Way," *The Martian Way and Other Stories* (New York: Ballantine, 1985): 41. This collection was first published in 1955
15. Ibid., 60
16. Asimov, *The Best of Isaac Asimov:* 12.
17. Asimov, "The Last Question," *Nine Tomorrows* (New York: Ballantine, 1985): 182-83. This collection was first published in 1959.
18. Asimov, "The Last Answer," *The Winds of Change and Other Stories* (New York: Doubleday, 1983): 160-61. This is the first publication of this collection.
19. Asimov, "The Last Shuttle," *The Winds of Change,* 164-65.
20. Asimov, "A Matter of Principle," *Isaac Asimov's Science Fiction Magazine,* February 1984: 30.
21. Ibid., 32.
22. Asimov, *The Alternate Asimovs* (New York: Doubleday, 1986): 269-70.
23. Asimov, "Originality," editorial, *Isaac Asimov's Science Fiction Magazine,* April 1986: 6. He says the article is entitled "If the Stars Appeared Only One Night in a Thousand Years" and was written by M.T. Brackbill. I have not seen the article. The relationship certainly invites more study.
24. Asimov, "Nightfall," *Nightfall and Other Stories* (Greenwich: Fawcett, 1969): 36. This collection was first published by Doubleday the same year.

III. CALVIN/ROBOT BOOKS AND THE FOUNDATION TRILOGY

One difficulty in describing the science fiction that Asimov continues to produce stems from his rational drive for coherence and unified generality. Like all "scientific" thinkers who have written after the methodological revolution of John Locke and the other reformers of the new science, Asimov can never leave his best ideas alone. He must continually elaborate and link new insights to old on the assumption that accumulated and interlocked knowledge is the only sort of valid knowledge. Moreover, Asimov denies the absolute insights of intuitive or "inspired" art by affirming the Lockean methodology of gradual accumulation. The images at the core of Asimov's fiction (robots and images of Empire are certainly part of that core) are not totally logical, transparent, and systematically arranged by himself. In spite of himself, this clear and coherent rationalist contacts depths of meaning that are sometimes not on the surface. In other words, the resonance in both *I, Robot* and *The Foundation Trilogy* seems significant, and that resonance or echoing is consistently from the 18th-century Enlightenment. Asimov may not be a conscious scholar of his roots in this context, though any critic would have to think carefully before maintaining positively that Asimov was not consciously aware of some idea. But it does help in understanding these remarkable and seminal longer fictions from the Campbell years to suggest their echoes from the Enlightenment.

One unifying device for *I, Robot* that Asimov uses to make a book out of nine stories from that first decade of fiction writing is the "life" of Dr. Susan Calvin. The other unifying device comes from the Three Laws of Robotics, which will be discussed after an examination of Susan Calvin's importance to the book. In his fine introduction to the whole canon of Asimovian science fiction up until the great outpouring in recent years of new Foundation and robot novels, James Gunn has worked out the "fixed-up" chronology for Calvin's life and spinster's career at U.S. Robots and Mechanical Men, Inc. and how that scientific career as "robopsychologist" interacts with key product robots and other employees. There had been other psychologists in the early short stories, even one or two that Asimov called "robopsychologists," and there certainly is the key role of psychohistory in the Foundation stories, but the unity in this book around Susan Calvin seems special.[1]

To piece together what was advertised in the early editions as a novel, Asimov wrote some linking sections to stories that, except for the first one that Frederik Pohl published, originally appeared in *Astounding*. The anthologist Groff Conklin, writing in an August 1952, "Foreword" to one of the early hardcover editions of the "novel," comments "...that is why Miss Calvin (whose name may have been chosen by the author with a wry eye on the significance of...Calvinism) is effective."[2] John Calvin, in fact, had laid out the general framework and time scheme that did much (paradoxically since Calvin himself was not a religious absolutist) to permit the gradualism of the secular Enlightenment and, ultimately, the technological and moral experimentation that Susan Calvin devotes her fictional existence to advancing.

Though too vast for discussion here, the libraries of scholarly literature that explain how the theology of Calvinistic predestination theory relates to the notion of the Puritan work ethic and thus to notions of gradualism and of progress would all be useful in understanding Asimov. However, the basic notion of Calvin's move to posit an immensely long time scheme along with built-in "uncertainty" about any one particular judgment or "election" that God might hand down, in fact, did much to liberate thinkers for the gradual experimentation necessary to modern science. This resolution fits Asimov perfectly although the theology itself is never his. He might prefer to invoke the immensely long and gradual history of Old Testament Hebrews, which does, in fact, seem calculated to postpone indefinitely any absolute appearance of final truth. The name Susan Calvin evokes for the reader the Puritan work ethic. She does work long and hard and is still not arrived at any absolute truth at the age of 82 when she dies. Asimov has commented in numerous places how he loves this character and has her say finally, "I will see no more. My life is over. You will see what comes next."[3] Verbs for seeing are no accident in the usage of an Enlightenment heroine.

Moreover, the adjectives used to describe the driven robopsychologist whose presence does so much for unifying *I, Robot* complement what Asimov correctly labels at the beginning of the book as her "cold enthusiasm"—"thin-lipped," "frosty pupils."[4]

Such ideological traits that she presumably shares with the other workers at U.S. Robots, and with Asimov himself, focus on virtues of control, pattern, predictability. Resonance, then, here is not only from the great advocate of complete control, John Calvin, but also from the secular determinist of the end of the 18th century, William Godwin.[5] Godwin's notion of "Necessity," which many critics have described in terms that resemble Calvinistic determinism rather than a strictly mechanistic determinism, seems to be echoed in the book's concluding story. The difference in the resonance is in a sort of moral imperative to the deterministic predictability, always present in Asimov, rather than just the predetermined motion of forces. In "The Evitable Conflict," benevolent machines seem able to anticipate and control *all* events in a way that sound much like the completeness of Necessity in Godwin. At the same time Susan Calvin's 'enthusiasm" is clear as she says finally:

". . .it means that the Machine is conducting our future for us not only simply in direct answer to our direct questions, but in general answer to the world situation and to human psychology as a whole. . . . Think, that for all time, all conflicts are finally evitable. Only the Machines, from now on, are inevitable."[6]

Asimov's youthful wordplay will grow into a more sophisticated wit in later novels where robotics play important roles, but his own celebration of generality and cool certainty seems clearly to be linked to Susan's here. To reach such high levels of reliable generality, Calvin and her U.S. Robots colleagues had to devise the simple calculus of the Three Laws of Robotics and, then, continually try out the balancing and interaction of the laws in all their combinations and permutations. Those continual games of "if this, then, the next" consume the stories in *I, Robot* and provide a further resonance with Godwinian Necessity. Not only is the general outcome of such a grand scheme as Necessity or the "Machines" completely reliable and determined but also the continual adjustments and "calculus" of the relations within the scheme are continually fascinating. It is as though Calvin, Asimov, and any such generalist and determinist have both nothing at stake and, at the same time, must always be making adjustments to their system. The belief in Necessity or in the overall general and benevolent outcome frees the "player," in fact, to manipulate the calculus of the game. Calvinistic theology, as well as Godwinian Necessity and Asimovian Robotics, liberate a sort of freeplay of will due to the most general sort of overall system. Such a paradox of free will existing within and because of a rigid system has no doubt been agonized over most by theologians, but echoes from Godwin to the Enlightenment Asimov do help the general reader understand the effects of the Susan Calvin narratives. Here is a key passage from Godwin writing about Necessity, both the determinism of it and the individual moves, which resound all through the cool, hard work of Susan Calvin in *I, Robot:*

> . . .if the doctrine of necessity do [sic] not annihilate virtue, it tends to introduce a great change into our ideas respecting it. . . . The believer in free-will can expostulate with, or correct, his pupil, with faint and uncertain hopes, conscious that the clearest exhibition of truth is impotent when brought into contest with the unhearing and indisciplinable faculty of will; or in reality, if he were consistent, secure that it could produce no effect. The necessarian on the contrary employs real antecedents, and has a right to expect real effects.[7]

Godwin's matter-of-fact dismissal of free will as just too absurdly random, indeed, suggests Asimov's firm ending to *I, Robot* with the notion that the machines control all reactions and even disguise this total control because, as benevolent robots, they know that a full realization of total control would cause mental anguish or "harm" to humans. Similarly, the three Laws themselves, or three "rules" of robotics as they are labeled in the first story where Asimov mentions them explicitly, "Runaround," seem hardly profound or a great invention of the imagination. They are neutral. Over the years, they have gone on to have almost a life of their own as "idea" outside of the fiction and are usually listed and worded with a sort of Godwinian flatness that hardly seems a great product of literature. Recently, they were invoked in a book collection of *Omni* essays on Robotics with their origin attributed to an Asimov novel written ten years later and with slight changes in punctuation and spelling.[8] It was in the 1942 *Astounding* story, however, in a dialogue between Powell and Donovan, who are the key "right stuff" associates of Calvin, that the Three Laws first appear:

> Powell's radio voice was tense in Donovan's ear: "Now, look, let's start with the three fundamental Rules of Robotics—the three rules that are built most deeply into a robot's positronic brain." In the darkness, his gloved fingers ticked off each point.
> "We have: One, a robot may not injure a human being, or, through inaction, allow a human being to come to harm."
> "Right!"
> "Two," continued Powell, "a robot must obey the orders given it by human beings except where such orders conflict with the First Law."

"Right!"

"And three, a robot must protect its own existence as long as such protection does not conflict with the First or Second Laws."

"Right! Now where are we?"[9]

Donovan and Powell could figure out exactly where they were and did solve their problem on Mercury, but it would take more robot stories and finally the book *I, Robot* itself for Asimov to know what a fine gimmick he had invented. Finally, he doctored all the stories in the "novel" so that they would be consistent with the Three Laws.

Further, just as Godwin paradoxically insists (like Calvin before him) that the believer in Necessity will work even harder to make things happen in this world, so Asimov's roboticists (and the robots themselves in his most recent fictions) never tire of discussing and trying to manipulate some implication of these three simple statements in relation to one another. A paradox is that the apparent certainty *liberates* near infinite permutations. Though, as in "Runaround," this continual balancing act often ". . .strikes an equilibrium [whereby]. . .Rule 3 drives him back and Rule 2 drives him forward," the permutations of all the robots seem like they will never end."[10] Thus the accomplishment is not only the general outcome of "control" but also the tinkering; it is a wonderful example of Asimov's inventiveness how complex and variable the Three Laws become.

Godwinian inclinations toward such clarity of analysis and such control may seem inhuman, even monstrous, so that Robotics itself, though the Laws are benevolent toward humans, assumes the effects of the very Frankenstein motif that Asimov was trying to avoid. It is the continual acknowledgment of the calculus of complexity, however, that keeps Asimov lively, benevolent, and "human" in his writing, especially his writing on the robots. He always is trying to teach and to clarify, and the material itself contains depths of complexity.

Asimov has continued to extrapolate on robotics and on the calculus of complexity from the simple three original Laws. Moreover, statements from both Asimov and Campbell can be found giving credit to one another for the original formulation of the Laws. It was, in fact, another natural and wonderful coaching job by the most important editor of the pulp magazines for one of his most receptive and gifted players.[11] Asimov himself says his favorite robot story is the longish and award-winning piece "The Bicentennial Man," first published in February 1976, some years after Campbell had died. Though the understated pathos in this story, in which a machine relentlessly moves toward "humanness" by arranging for its own death, seems uncharacteristic of the cooler speculation over permutations in the Laws that precede and follow it, Asimov demonstrates a fictional versatility that would have pleased Campbell.

Most recently, Asimov has gathered and rearranged all of his thirty-one robot short stories from 1939 to 1977 in *The Complete Robot* (1982). The initial Susan Calvin gathering in 1950, however, still has the greater charm as a book. Further, it demonstrates how intensely Asimov wanted to generalize and expand the ideas he was producing as magazine fiction for Campbell and how suitable these ideas were for repetition and variation. In other words, the young Asimov was ready with book-length ideas when the post-war marketplace was ready for science-fiction books.

The series of stories dealing with the Foundations that was evolving at the same time as the robot series in the decade of the forties is not only the fiction for which Asimov is best known but also, perhaps, is the best example of his inclinations toward the general and, in this case, toward the human and toward storytelling. In addition to his numerous autobiographical reminiscences about this remarkable invention of *The Foundation Trilogy,* Asimov's 1953 venture into full-fledged literary criticism with his essay for Reginald Bretnor entitled "Social Science Fiction" is both close enough to the actual writing of the stories and candid enough to be very helpful. Asimov has become increasingly more coy about doing literary criticism himself—perhaps he has come to see more clearly and to take more seriously hard science-fiction writing as radical and important. As *The Foundation Trilogy* was first appearing in book form, what he had to say about the genre in general reveals a great deal about what he himself had accomplished by that time and about his set of mind with its debt to the Enlightenment. First of all, he effectively disassociates himself from the "gadget" materialism of science-fiction writers by defining what he and Campbell have been interested in as the influence of social change and history: "people movement" rather than "gadgets." Second, Asimov makes clear in this essay both his knowledge of the revolutionary changes that took place in the 18th century and his admiration for the "discovery of history" that had not been truly possible prior to the Enlightenment because humans had not experienced fundamental change:

> . . .if science fiction is to deal with fictitious societies as possessing potential reality rather

than as being nothing more than let's-pretend object lessons, it must be post-Napoleonic. Before 1789 human society didn't change as far as the average man was concerned and it was silly, even wicked, to suppose it could. After 1815, it was obvious to any educated man that human society not only could change but that it did.[12]

The fact that the young chemistry student at Columbia read as much history as he did is remarkable in itself. Later, in the 1953 essay, he identifies more fully this continuing fascination with the details of human history that provided story outlines for narratives in the *Trilogy:* "I wrote other stories, the germs of whose ideas I derived from the histories of Justinian and Belisarius, Tamerlane and Bajazet, John and Pope Innocent III."[13] L. Sprague de Camp speaks of their "Toynebean period" at the end of the "foundation" decade, and Asimov himself recollects that, when he originally proposed to Campbell a tale about the fall of a Galactic Empire and a return to feudalism, it seemed perfectly natural to him since he "had read Gibbon's *Decline and Fall of the Roman Empire* not once but twice." Such extensive youthful reading may be exaggerated; both statements are reminiscences on the occasion of Asimov most recently returning to the series, but there is no question that, whereas the recent sequels fuse with the robot novels and introduce other themes, the original *Trilogy* has an overwhelming soaking from Gibbon, Toynbee, and the whole sweep of history seen from the perspective of a remarkable young man's readings.[14]

In addition to this fascination with cycles in Toynbee, with pessimism in Gibbon, and with the whole detailed sweep of Roman history as it moved from repeating intrigue to resistance to forward movement to second-stage collapse, Asimov also knew *Old Testament* history This history creates for him the same patterns as it moved into Roman history, with the Maccabean wars, and eventually fused with the building of the Christian church inside the Roman Empire. Certainly the continuing sense of exile and lament for a destroyed Jerusalem suggests the lost glory of Trantor as much as a fallen Rome does. The early church hidden within the declining Empire is a sort of "type and symbol" for the second foundation even if Gibbon would not agree. Also, mutant and mule-like leaders keep emerging all through ancient history: Alexander, Jesus, Julian. The main point here is not to insist on specific parallels; I have neither the scholarship nor the time. However, history itself, and specifically the future history modeled on the reading of history as it has been known since the Enlightenment, must be acknowledged, first, as the major theme in these foundation stories that epitomize Asimov's own description of social science fiction.

In other words, the vision of open-ended possibility and the full recognition of "change' in society that so characterized the revolution of the Enlightenment, which Asimov talks about in his 1953 essay and images in the *Trilogy*, manifests itself not only in the permutations and analyses of robotics but also in the realization of the nature of history itself. The record of human history, written from Gibbon and Hume to the 19th-century historical scholars of the Bible to Asimov himself, contains nothing that can be called "absolute." Rather it recounts continuing movement from one faction to another, by spurts and long fallow declines, and repeated variations on the images of equilibrium and disequilibrium.

Just as one can see few absolute truths in the panorama of change and history, so Asimov's texts are never set in stone. He does seem perfectly comfortable with the publishing practices that made up the commercial "relativism" of pulp science fiction. Whereas a Joyce text or other examples of nostalgic "high art" in our scientific age would be early standardized to be set in type the same way each time as they were "absolute," Asimov had to accept a more fluid state of the text affecting *The Foundation Trilogy* even after the stories had become books. For example, the first novel becomes *The 1,000-Year Plan* in a drastically cut 1955 edition that sold for a quarter. Asimov did not seem to mind. Further, as his career has gone on and scientific knowledge and terminology have changed, Asimov updates his texts. This would seem to confirm that he finds little of permanence or absoluteness in art when science itself changes so rapidly. In his essay "The Story Behind 'Foundation,'" which he wrote to introduce the surge of sequel writing which began to appear in 1982, Asimov anticipates new scientific findings that he can now incorporate into the narrative:

> The Foundation series had been written at a time when our knowledge of astronomy was primitive compared with what it is today. I could take advantage of that and at least *mention* black holes, for instance. I could also include electronic computers, which had not been invented until I was half through with the series.[15]

Even before the sequel writing, however, he was quietly changing throughout the *Trilogy* the word "atomic" to read "nuclear" when he refers to the new form of energy that has come to be renamed in the years since the Second World War. Scholars of the future are bound to have particular troubles with the texts and the setting of the texts for science fiction works if the attempt is ever made to "establish" them as high art and thus to standardize a text.[16]

Though neither history nor art itself is able to supply the absolute Truths we think they might, nevertheless, *The Foundation Trilogy* brims with general ideas and themes that momentarily and in their mutability do catch the imagination as substitutes for absolutism. More than the continual variations on political or military intrigue in the plot, which echo continual intrigue in history itself, these general themes woven into the *Trilogy* are what affect the reader. The most important themes are, in fact, representative of the rational urge in Asimov to move always to the general itself. These emerge from the overall tale of Hari Seldon's plan through the "science" of psychohistory to lessen the chaotic effects of declining control within the Galactic Empire and to establish a new "Enlightenment" by means of the First Foundation that he institutes on the planet Terminus, working in a continuing tension with the Second Foundation.

The first general idea is an echo not so much of the fall of the Roman Empire, though the hidden and ameliorative influence of the early Church may be a "foundation" resonance here, as it is a set of images from the 18th-century Enlightenment. Certainly the major activity of the Seldon psychohistorians is work on the *Encyclopedia Galactica,* which is quoted from periodically throughout the *Trilogy*. The echo is to the massive French work, done also by a small army of new scientists that helped both to overthrow the *ancien regime* in the 18th century and to "enlighten" the effects of darkness following the decline of that Empire. However, history itself, or the whole record of human activity over time, is also the theme of these future *encyclopedistes*. The important effect is the general notion about history that is stated perhaps most clearly in *Foundation and Empire*, the second book, though it is implicit in the entire set of stories. Here is an expression of the consternation felt by the villain Bel Riose in the face of Necessity:

> Riose's voice trembled with indignation. "You mean that this art of his predicts that I would attack the Foundation and lose such and such a battle for such and such a reason? You are trying to say that I am a silly robot following a predetermined course into destruction."
> "No," replied the old patrician, sharply. "I have already said that the science had nothing to do with individual actions. It is the vaster background that has been foreseen."
> "Then we stand clasped tightly in the forcing hand of the Goddess of Historical Necessity."
> "Of *Psycho*-Historical Necessity," prompted Barr, softly.[17]

There is sadness in such "determinism" for the individual actor, and that sadness is the second major general idea to consider. In a real way, also, it is simply another facet of the image of decline that is inevitable over vast stretches of time. It is the same sublime sense of cycles that gave such energy to "Nightfall" and that Asimov indeed found validated in his readings of the historians from Hume and Gibbon on, even to the great events of the Second World War that he was experiencing. When cycles themselves and vast wars are the main "heroes" in history, individuals like Bel Riose do indeed feel overshadowed. Such a sense of eclipse and small "modernness" can be seen best in the key villain of the *Trilogy,* the mutant and sad man who is able to alter emotions, and whom Asimov strangely named the Mule. Gunn has noted how much Asimov did seem to like this character of the Mule, and it is evident in the fact that, except for Hari Seldon and his "plan," the Mule figures in more stories than any other individual.[18] His very role of enemy to all other forces in the Galaxy, including the Foundation, ambiguously combined with his ability, by means of antagonist acts, to promote the eventual benevolent outcomes of the Seldon Plan illustrate the predetermined sense of destiny conquering time that causes all "moderns" at any given time to experience the Mule's sense of sadness. Humanity does not have the control he would like. To hint, again, at an *Old Testament* reading for Asimov's sweep of future history rather than the usual Roman one, the Mule (like the "Assyrian") is the "servant of the Lord" as he punishes a vainglorious Israel; similarly, all the vast sweep of Hebrew history is continually sad.

The second important theme, then, is nostalgia for the lost glory of individual heroism, balanced nicely with a full acceptance and celebration of smaller, limited "modernness." In fact, this is the motif of the Ancients versus the Moderns or the lament for lost Golden Ages coupled with the realization of the advantages in an Iron Age. I think Asimov also learned this from the Enlightenment. It is the Georgic mode that pervades so much 18th-century literature in which men were coming to terms with the complexities and limits of the peculiar "modernness" following the scientific revolution and the Glorious Revolution.[19] Regardless of how deeply scholarship can measure this resonance, however, the theme seems clear in the *Trilogy*. The Mule is a strangely limited leader. He spends much of his time in the disguise of the court fool Magnifico, in fact; sadly, like his namesake, he is lonely and infertile. In other words, "Moderns" are small and limited compared to the "Ancients."

Similarly, the Iron Age adaptability of the Foundation itself seems well implemented by Asimov to contrast with the glory of Empire. Nuclear devices must be small in the Foundation. Traders and other leaders are always somewhat imperfect and ineffectual as individuals; only the Plan itself is ultimately effective. This would almost seem like an emblem for social reality in the modern age, in which lost glories are always in the past and humanity must cope with limited means in the present. Further, the Foundation itself is always working far out and on the periphery of the Galaxy, and even the Second Foundation located at the other "end" is hidden and small. This translation, which Asimov cleverly makes of the cycles of history and of the spiral shape of the Galaxy into the mysterious loops that eventually bring readers to discover the Second Foundation back on Trantor, suggests the non-heroic peripheral details of a "modern" technological age. Or to jump to the *Old Testament* again, the Lord moves in mysterious ways; one of the most mysterious is that grand results are accomplished by means of small, peripheral, modern people.

A final overall theme returns to the role of generalization and to the centrality of humans. Though it is significant that a concluding heroine in this massive narrative is a writer, the future novelist Arkady Darell, just as a journalist is a key point of view character in "Nightfall," the real hero is the sublime history of humanity itself. It is this large vision, which only the Enlightenment could take, that ultimately submerges even the individual heroism of the writer into the sadness mentioned above. However, the more important way to conceptualize this effect is in terms of the general idea itself. (In this way, the thought of William Godwin, who was after all also a novelist, is further seen as a key prototype.) Here is Hari Seldon, himself, speaking at his trial that provides the focus for the shorter initial piece that Asimov wrote last as the book publication was being readied:

> "I shall not be alive half a decade hence," said Seldon, "and yet it [the future] is of overpowering concern to me. Call it idealism. Call it an identification of myself with that mystical generalization to which we refer by the term, 'man.'"[20]

When he writes the later sequels, Asimov will have his robot heroes come back to this big generalization about "'man.'" The important thing to see, then, is his move again to the large general idea. Therefore, just as *I, Robot* toys with permutations in laws that echo Godwinian Necessity, so the early Foundation stories support this paradoxically liberating vision with the added notion of a vast, yet anthropocentric history.

NOTES

1. For the chronology and a useful summary discussion, see James Gunn's *Isaac Asimov: The Foundations of Science Fiction* (New York: Oxford UP, 1982): 54 ff.

2. Groff Conklin, "Foreword," *I, Robot* by Isaac Asimov (New York: Grosset & Dunlap, n.d.). The Foreword is dated "August 1952" and appears on an unnumbered page. Recently in an editorial for the magazine that bears his name, Asimov explains how he came up with her name and denies all Calvinism. See Asimov, "Susan Calvin," editorial, *Isaac Asimov's Science Fiction Magazine,* December 1982: 7-12.
3. Asimov, *I, Robot* (New York: Ballantine, 1983): 192. A fine, recent discussion of Calvinism and science fiction with reference to the "hardness" in Asimov is David Clayton's "What Makes Hard Science Fiction 'Hard'?" in *Hard Science Fiction,* ed. George E. Slusser and Eric S. Rabkin (Carbondale: Southern Illinois UP, 1986): 58-69.
4. *I, Robot,* "Introduction" and 171.
5. See my section on William Hazlitt and the notion of the future in my *Comic Tones in Science Fiction* (Westport, CT: Greenwood, 1982): 40 ff.
6. *I, Robot,* 192.
7. William Godwin, *Enquiry Concerning Political Justice and Its Influence on Morals and Happiness* (1793) in *Backgrounds of Romanticism,* ed. Leonard M. Trawick (Bloomington: Indiana UP, 1967): 211-12.
8. See T.A. Heppenheimer, "Man Makes Man," in *Robotics,* ed. Marvin Minsky (Garden City, NY: Doubleday, 1985): 49-51.
9. *I, Robot,* 40.
10. Ibid., 41.
11. See Asimov, *In Memory Yet Green: The Autobiography of Isaac Asimov, 1920-1954* (Garden City, NY: Doubleday, 1979): 285-87.
12. Asimov, "Social Science Fiction," in *Science Fiction: The Future,* ed. Dick Allen (New York: Harcourt Brace, 1971): 266-67. The essay was first published in Bretnor's *Modern Science Fiction* in 1953.
13. Ibid., 278.
14. L. Sprague de Camp, "Commentary," *Isaac Asimov's Science Fiction Magazine,* December 1982: 62.
15. Asimov, "The Story Behind the 'Foundation,'" *Isaac Asimov's Science Fiction Magazine,* December 1982: 41.

16. Note, also, that in the 1983 Ballantine paperback edition of *Foundation,* the word "explosion" in regard to a "nuclear" disaster is now "meltdown." Compare earlier editions with page 60 in the 1983 edition.
17. Asimov, *Foundation and Empire* (New York: Avon, 1966): 29.
18. Gunn, 139.
19. See my essay "Asimov's Golden Age: The Ordering of an Art," in *Isaac Asimov,* ed. Joseph D. Olander and Martin Harry Greenberg (New York: Taplinger, 1977): 111-19.
20. Asimov, *Foundation* (New York: Avon, 1966): 31.

IV. THREE EARLY NOVELS AND THE JUVENILES

Both the tone of "sadness" in Asimov's grand vision of psychohistory, highlighted at the end of the previous chapter, as well as his ongoing moves to fill in details to his general scheme, are important redeeming qualities in his "futurism," or future history. This vision of a future history has come under major attack. At the midpoint in this examination of his career, then, I need to consider the most rigorous and serious objection to the early accomplishment of the Foundation vision. Further, an understanding and qualification of this objection will serve to develop more fully Asimov's use of the general idea and to introduce discussion of a body of book-length fictions from the Fifties written with the Foundation vision in mind.

When Charles Elkins published his essay entitled "Isaac Asimov's 'Foundation' Novels: Historical Materialism Distorted into Cyclical Psycho-History" in 1976, Asimov's reputation was certainly large enough to justify the celebration accorded the essay by its editor: "It was time to say that 'the King is naked'—that is what Elkins does soundly and rigorously."[1] Acknowledging that the popularity of the *Trilogy* may be due to images in the novels that resemble "a vulgar Marxist version of historical materialism," Elkins concludes:

> ... Asimov's failure to grasp the complexities of historical materialism and the humanistic emphasis of Marxism constitutes their [the novels'] major intellectual and artistic deficiency.[2]

Specifically, Elkins points out that the fatalism in Asimov's vision reduces individual human action and understanding more than Marx and Engels ever intended and, in fact, does not allow for any progress, or even change, in history. Strangely, as in Calvinism itself, Elkins argues, few concrete evidences ever are available about what actually will happen in the future in Asimov, so that the Seldon Plan humanity plugs along with little information other than "faith" in the Plan. Worst of all, an elite fascism of Foundation experts militates against the individual. Elkins accuses Asimov of wanting a rule by experts and the hard technology of a Heinlein. This last point should suggest that the Asimov that Elkins reads is a very different thinker from the rather radical man of the Enlightenment who is opposed to expert elitism and always in favor of the open-ended idea.[3]

The crux to this difference of interpretation is the matter of detail in history and the possibilities for change. Though he does cite the ideas about change in Asimov's 1953 essay on social science fiction, Elkins emphasizes that Galactic Empire man from 12,000 years in the future seems no different from modern humanity. Thus, the key issue has to do with images of change, with the epistemology of change, and with Asimov's use of detail. The consideration of other novels from the Fifties should help resolve more clearly this image of Asimov the generalist, even the secular Calvinist, who does continually want to fill in details but never so many details that the resulting complexity of observation will be at the expense of his "faith." This is, indeed, the image of the amateur with an open-ended vision of possibility for mankind. Thus belief in the Seldon Plan, like Godwinian Necessity and philosophic anarchy, entails a concept of something like an "invisible hand" that must never be an expert managing hand despite what Asimov's avidly conforming characters believe. Perhaps a key difference between classic *laissez-faire* economics and Marxist ideas is that the Marxist presumes more expert control. Paradoxically, even Asimov's thorough professionalism as a writer was formed at key points by the invisible hand of circumstance. The man himself and his career may, in fact, reflect the theme of non-expert control, of the notion of philosophic anarchy that Godwin envisioned as the overall order of Necessity. Asimov is a lucky amateur in some ways.

Moreover, part of the sense of change is the realization that the present always remains distinct from the past and the future, cut off and different from both. Asimov's voice in his continuing present, longing for the past and the future, is his recognition of change. I think it is significant, as mentioned in the previous chapter, that the text of the Foundation stories has been updated by Asimov to reflect changing terminology in science. (The implications of such practice do, in fact, raise questions about the high-art status and verisimilitude of any literature and may be among the most subversive elements in science fiction.) Actually, *Pebble in the Sky* does use some names to hint at the evolution of Earth language during the millennia between the twentieth century and the Galactic Empire: Chicago becomes "Chica" and St. Louis "Senloo." However, Asimov never presumes a fiction in which language creation is absolute so that he, the artist, might create the language of the Galactic Empire. Rather it is theme and idea, along with his voice as pulp writer, that he used to convey the sense of change. In no place other than in the continually expanding set of fictions on his future history that fill in bits and pieces of events in the

Galactic Empire, both before and after the fall, does he better play the theme of origins and of change and of the painful comparison between the Ancients and the Moderns.

Certainly his autobiographical urge, also, may be seen as part of this development of the sublime theme of change through history that is often ruled by an invisible hand rather than by experts. *The Alternate Asimovs* volume, which recently has made available the previously unpublished shorter version of *Pebble in the Sky*, exists not only for commercial overkill but also to uncover more of the record of Asimov's own history. Sometimes he cannot resist changing a small item just to make himself look better, but that urge of ego may also be seen as part of the invisible hand of history. The overall effect is order. What may look like a mistake at any given present is seen later as part of the plan. Elkins undoubtedly will label this autobiographical complacency as blind fatalism, but it does seem to be a dominant operating principle and strength both in Asimov's life and his fiction. The rejected early version of the story carried the title "Grow Old with Me," which misquotes the opening line of Robert Browning's poem "Rabbi ben Ezra"; Asimov silently corrects this to the proper wording "Grow Old Along with Me" in *The Alternate Asimovs*, but fully acknowledges what a lucky circumstance it was that his 1947 text was rejected.[4] A year and a half later, he expanded the story, and *Pebble in the Sky* became his first published novel, appearing from Doubleday in January 1950. As usual, Asimov was working hard, but an invisible hand was helping as well.

One of the most uncanny and effective elements in all of Asimov's fiction, and one which illustrates this notion of the invisible hand, is the interweaving of his favorite general themes along with his constant preparation for, and receptiveness to, this web. Like the Seldon Plan itself and the work of the Foundations, such a thematic web could never have been totally managed by Asimov. Rather it is the "root and ground" of his storytelling that reaches way back, as Algis Budrys suggests, at least as far as "Black Friar of the Flame."[5] Asimov is aware of this thematic web continually; he builds on it and, in the latest sequels, continues to build on it, rationally. However, he seems to have set it up from the start in an uncanny and lucky way. If setting and overall "surround" are in themselves key fictional elements in science fiction that separate it from other literature, as Gregory Benford has recently repeated, then for Asimov the resonance of his large ideas is part of his setting.[6] James Gunn argues that plot itself is the most important element, and he paraphrases in his usual thorough and clear way what he identifies as the more intricate plot of *Pebble in the Sky*:

> The plot is more complicated than usual for Asimov fiction. The story develops along several simultaneous lines, beginning with the accidental translation (by means of an unrelated laboratory incident) of a sixty-two-year-old retired tailor named Joseph Schwartz to an Earth thousands of years in the future.[7]

This future Earth is a small province among an incredibly large number of inhabited planets in the 827th year of the same Galactic Empire that would later produce Hari Seldon. One of the lines of plot, which eventually Schwartz himself manages to foil when he is finally persuaded to accept the "ecumenicalism" of Empire across the Galaxy, turns on militant resentment and a scheme to destroy the Empire. Part of this resentment, of course, is due to the sense of oppression that provinces feel in an empire (*e.g.*, Judea under Roman rule). More fundamentally, the resentment derives from a hazy and lost intuition about origins and about the lack of proper recognition for origins. Like the ancient Hebrews, Asimov's Earthpeople of Galactic Era 827 do feel a strong intuition that everything important in civilization originated with them, but the origins have been lost in the distant past. The real hero in this story is not even the setting of a radioactively charred Earth where dystopian measures such as euthanasia have evolved, but rather the sense of scope itself—the sense of origins. As we shall see, Asimov will never abandon this wonderful theme of the Ancients versus the Moderns, of Oedipal priorities, and of lost knowledge. What is doubly wonderful is that he set it for himself as early as 1947, and even earlier, since lost knowledge is also the problem in his story "Nightfall."

On Earth in the ninth century of the Galactic Empire, fading hints of the true origins are jealously maintained by the Society of Ancients. At the same time and working from the opposite direction, Imperial scientists are theorizing and investigating along lines that will prove futile for the time being, since it is known that, during the Foundations, Earth is totally obscured in cultural memory. Nevertheless, here is Asimov's description of the work of the archaeologist Bel Arvardan, another of his fine Enlightenment characters groping for the Truth:

> Arvardan. . .uncovered traces of the early civilization. . .and proved that the earliest rec-

ords of the planet [elsewhere in the Galaxy—his goal is to prove that humans radiated outward from a source rather than evolved separately] showed traces of interstellar trade. The final touch came when he demonstrated beyond any doubt that Man had emigrated to the region in an already civilized state.

It was after this that the *J. Gal. Arch. Soc.* (to give the Journal its professional abbreviation) decided to print Arvardan's Senior Dissertation more than ten years after it had been presented.

And now the pursuit of his pet theory led Arvardan to probably the least significant planet of the Empire—the planet called Earth.[8]

The big story is not so much in the intrigues or reversals of plot as in the quest for origins. Asimov will hold that investigation open and is still using the theme in his most recent fictions. Arvardan's research, however, was conceived and appears in nearly the same wording in the earlier 1947 text of the story—echoes of Asimov as doctoral student worried about the reception of his own research. The earlier version of the story is told, also, in divided sections that introduce first the Schwartz story and then the Arvardan story.[9] When he expanded them to novel length in 1949, Asimov wove the stories together and eliminated some precious and clumsy first-person asides to the reader. So, although his themes and his inclinations had been from the start toward the large general ideas that had supported his Robot and his Foundation series, it did take some effort to learn to produce novel-length narratives as originals.

During the winter of 1949-50, he went on to produce his second long manuscript of this type; both he and Gunn agree that the resulting novel is his least satisfactory narrative. In *The Stars, Like Dust,* Asimov "committed the customary sin of the sophomore novel."[10] The judgments of "cardboard" characterization made by Elkins are painfully applicable in this story where the move to transpose conventions from the western "horse opera" into space opera results in character names such as the "Rancher of Widemos" and where government progress in the Galaxy rests on the rediscovery of a copy of the United States' Constitution (a touch suggested by the editor Horace Gold for the serialization in *Galaxy*).[11] Nevertheless, Asimov's intuition in this novel is to continue to shape his theme on origins and to build his sense of cohesiveness yet strangeness in the history of the Galaxy.

Brian Aldiss has recently argued that images of Galactic Empire are shallow and unconvincing and, as such, are apparently cover-ups for weak and muddled thinking. This attack echoes the praise in Elkins of the great, systematic thinkers on historical processes, over against what he characterizes as the shallow Galactic "imperialists." Aldiss goes on to speculate, rightly I think, that a true image for Galactic Empire must include the attempt to forge a collective consciousness that would serve as the real link among all the parts of such a system.[12] Aldiss does mention Asimov, but neither he nor Elkins does justice to the main effect in these Galactic Empire novels (the three non-juvenile novels discussed in this chapter are now marketed as the "Galactic Empire Novels"). This is also the effect that Asimov tries to weave into other series and, as some say, now into the whole canon of his work. In fact, the move toward exactly what Aldiss identifies as the need for a collective consciousness is one of the few redeeming qualities in the otherwise silly story of *The Stars, Like Dust*. Another is the "gadget" description of space navigation, which assumes in this novel the intensity of a Hal Clement expertise, but Asimov is never working just for gadget effects.[13]

The "western" plot in this novel involves the defeat of "cattle-baron" type villains on the planet Tyrann (again, Gold suggested that strange pun as the title for the serialization and Asimov unfortunately agreed). The point in future history is long before the Galactic Empire has evolved and when the original Earth is still well remembered. Asimov writes best when he is remembering what has been lost, and the common origin and common memories represent his accumulative construction of a viable collective consciousness. As they talk over tactics, here is recollection from a wise old adviser to the young hero, whose father has been murdered in the "range war," about what is really important in the continuing story of the Galaxy:

> All the Galaxy has been in a continuing state of expansion since the first discovery of interstellar travel. We have always been a growing society, therefore an immature society. It is obvious that human society reached maturity in only one place and at only one time and that this was on Earth immediately prior to its catastrophe. . . . We have lost much or all of that and it is a pity. Now here's an amusing thing. When Hinrik was a young man, he was a great Primitivist. He had a library on things Earthly that was unparalleled in the galaxy. . . . In a way, I've inherited it. Their literature, such scraps as survive, is fascinating. It has a peculiarly introspective flavor to

it that we don't have in our extraverted Galactic civilization.[14]

Earlier one of the "cowboy" characters, thoroughly extraverted in the Galactic sense of power struggles leading eventually to Empire, who despises the charred "pebble" of Earth, speaks with some impatience about the cohesive origin notions: "It is always very fashionable to assume that there are lost arts and lost sciences, and there are always these people who make a cult of primitivism and who make all sorts of ridiculous claims for the prehistoric civilizations on Earth."[15] The point is that Asimov focuses frequently in his space adventures on just such images so that the theme of origins itself becomes not only a unifying device in these novels but also Asimov's image for a driving force in Empire.

Further, one characteristic for Asimov of the seat of origins on Earth is the luminous, impossible notion (a Golden Age notion, in fact) of full maturity and introspection just prior to the "catastrophe." He does not specify exactly what the catastrophe is, leaving it open for later sequels. However, in *Pebble in the Sky* he had already set post-catastrophic Earth aglow with radioactivity. Now in the third novel, which he wrote immediately in succession in this set, he can hit on an image and a character derived from this "glowing" condition. The new mysterious sort of character he creates opens up not only more suggestions about lost Golden Age implications, which surely must be cohesive as civilization moves outward with Iron Age extraversion, but also scientific speculations on cosmological origins.

The Currents of Space (1952) is much better as a strong speculative narrative than its predecessor. It is a rich book and a fine culmination to the Galactic Empire novels before Asimov was to move on, for the time being, to novels on robotics and other matters. Also, it is significant that in the reissues of this novel, as well as each of the other Galactic Empire novels, Asimov qualifies the scientific speculations he had made when he wrote them. In particular, the levels of tolerable radioactivity on Earth and the cosmology of "carbon currents" as effecting nova formation in this latter novel are disclaimed by the scientist who is always aware of changing data, but the images are kept by the writer partly because they are images for change.

Set in the available time slot just before the Trantorian Republic of planets prevails in all the petty power struggles and expands to Empire, *The Currents of Space* both celebrates the Iron Age triumph of a *pax Trantorian* and reflects mysterious Golden Age epistemology of how to know things that cannot be known. Again, Asimov seems more interested in the epistemology than in the power politics among the planets, just as psychohistory is more an image to excite his imagination than warfare is in the Foundation stories. An Earthman who has grown up strange and troubled, partly because of the radioactivity (but the implication is that all those who long for lost Golden Ages are strange in the "extraverted" Galaxy of Iron), becomes a member of the small "foundation-like" group of intellectuals called the Interstellar Spatio-analytic Bureau. He then becomes even more lost and strange when a new discovery he has made causes him to be exiled and "mind-wiped." Crazy Rik, as he comes to work for the cause of the threatened planet Florina and to regain his powers of spatio-analysis, represents a fascinating character at the core of the novel. It is an epistemological core in which non-extravert and lost people reach for hidden meanings. Much as psychohistory or the puzzles of deterministic Necessity represent intellectual methodologies that are also mysterious, the art of spatio-analysis, which in this case is triggered by a nearly forgotten and radioactive Earth, probes what cannot be known. The slogan for the Institute that nurtured Rik, in fact, is "We Analyze Nothing."

So Asimov the hard scientist, who disclaims theories once he knows the facts are against them and who updates his terminology to fit scientific change, is also Asimov the prober into mystery and the image maker, pursuing a sense of origins and a Golden Age locus that might provide the consciousness to hold together a Galaxy. Finally, in this novel that anticipates and celebrates the ecumenical triumph of Trantor, a backward look to the language of origin is, also, most functional. The wily old senior spatio-analyst will work for Empire but also will speculate backward to origins. In this case the origins have to do both with language and with racism because Asimov's point of view character here is Black:

> When Dr. Junz left Libair for the Arcturian Institute of Spatial Technology and later entered his profession, the early fairy tales were forgotten. Only once since then had he really wondered. He had happened upon one of the ancient worlds of the Centuarian Sector in the course of business; one of those worlds whose history could be counted in millennia and whose language was so archaic that its dialect must almost be that lost and mythical language, English. They had a special word for a man with dark skin.[16]

Again, Asimov knows enough about the scope of change not to try to imitate specific changes that language might undergo. More presumptuous high-art writers might invoke something like the permanence of human nature and then attempt to map evolving languages. Asimov creates the scope of change itself, in part by means of the images for lost origins and lost Golden Ages.

It would involve more theory than this short guide to all his science fiction can find space for to resolve whether the more "mature" literature is the high art of sensing permanence or the rather broad summoning of change so vast that much is lost. However, Asimov's harshest critics often seem to have resolved this question that they fault him, as well as at times the science-fiction genre as a whole, for being too adolescent or juvenile. The implication throughout Elkins' essay, in fact, is that Asimov is juvenile in his lapses and his uncertainties and that, indeed, this stance represents an adolescent cover-up of base traits, such as the desire for a blatant fascism. Elkins is not alone. The recent probing essay by David Clayton in the nicely titled volume *Hard Science Fiction* argues that "hard" for Asimov and Robert A. Heinlein means a tough, paranoidlike, defensive position against all the forces of nature in which Heinlein's "capable man," in particular, operates as a sort of nervous, immature vigilante.[17] In Asimov's work, perhaps the images of Galactic Empire building are adolescent and wish-fulfillment efforts to forge a shallow collective consciousness or, more pathologically, a juvenile search for the father that opens the searcher to a historical domination by his worst inner forces of aggression and muddled thinking.

However, Asimov's writing strategies, though they may be as wrong-headed as Elkins would have it, usually are consistent and well stocked with example. So this question of juvenile effects can be met directly by considering the six juvenile novels that Asimov wrote in the Fifties, beginning in March 1951.[18] He originally used the pseudonym Paul French since the scheme, that he and Pohl, as agent, and Doubleday hoped would work out, was a television series with echoes of *The Lone Ranger* radio series. Also, Gunn argues that these "Space Ranger" stories are even more gadget-oriented, with the emphasis on instruction in basic science for young people, than other juveniles and that they lack the intrinsic unity of theme as in the Heinlein stories about the capable man.[19] However, these six *Lucky Starr* books are unified by the same images and themes as the Galactic Empire novels and with even greater resonance, perhaps, for a collective consciousness because clearly they are juveniles written energetically for young audiences, for a Golden Age.

Further, an intrinsic unity that is sustained throughout Asimov's writing of these juvenile novels, perhaps as a sort of residual effect from his Foundation stories and from the Galactic novels, centers on the notion of generation in all of its depth of meaning. The "generation" of a Galaxy-wide civilization is certainly a grandiose, adolescent sort of idea, and the word itself (though in Asimov the effect is always more from the idea than from "the word") evokes the profound pun on generation in poems by William Butler Yeats, especially in the one with overtones of the juvenile, "Among School Children."[20] Yeats properly uses the word to refer both to creating or generating new things and to an awareness of loss and age differences among the "generations." Thus the position of Asimov's juveniles in his career and the natural linking he incorporates into them between the Galactic future history, which had absorbed him through much of his writing, and the "Golden Age" of Earth and the Solar System as origin, give them a unity and resonance that need to be noticed.

In other words, all six books are set in the Golden Age of Earth before the great "radioactive" catastrophe and fictionally carry within them the generating origins of both robotics and Galactic expansion. Actually, the time slot is somewhat later than that of his short story from the Fifties, "The Martian Way," which is idyllic in its tone of hopefulness for expansion into space because human settlement has reached beyond the Solar System to the Sirius System where the villains, in fact, are based. This is also roughly the time slot of the Robot novels, written in this period and examined in the next chapter, that focus in a more sophisticated way on smaller, "adult" effects of characterization and style, as David Samuelson has pointed out.[21] Whether in adolescent images of scope and generation or in more detailed writing for adults, this writing period was Asimov's own Golden Age; so his development of his fictional Golden Age in the future history of Earth seems particularly appropriate.

The young, visionary hero who thinks eloquently about mankind going to the stars in "The Martian Way," Ted Long, had lost his parents in a space accident.[22] Similarly, David Starr, the space ranger, has been orphaned in space. Also, Asimov opens the juvenile stories with a setting on Mars and, again as in the short story, makes the point that humanity on Mars is becoming different. "Gravity legs" are different. Asimov writes about Martian "farmboys" (like the "ranchers" in *The Stars, Like Dust*). Even though David Starr and his Martian sidekick, Bigman, talk out together a lot of science instruction for young people, the overall effect of their characters is a nice balance and mix of youthful energy "generating" the future and the sense of orphaned difference or lostness.

Contributing to Asimov's tendency, which disturbs Elkins so thoroughly, toward images that suggest a fatalistic transfer of control to some secret Foundation-like force (the invisible hand supporting the whole scope of future history) is the Council of Science that Starr works for in all the stories:

> In these days, when science really permeated all human society and culture, scientists could no longer restrict themselves to their laboratories. It was for that reason that the Council of Science had been born. Originally it was intended only as an advisory body to help the government on matters of galactic importance, where only trained scientists could have sufficient information to make intelligent decisions. More and more it had become a crime-fighting agency, a counterespionage system. . . . Through its activities there might grow, someday, a great Empire of the Milky Way in which all men might live in peace and harmony.[23]

This Council seems a clear predecessor of the secret Foundations, and as it extends its work beyond "science," it evokes the hopes and dreams of the illusory "Golden Age"—always either lost in the past or fading into the future. Also, like the deep sense of lostness that any orphan will feel, the order of Empire always is precarious, even for juveniles. Here is Lucky Starr letting down his youthful, "generative" guard for a moment and pondering the other side of generation, inevitable loss: "He felt a twinge of homesickness and then a new resolve to keep war away from the teeming billions of human beings that inhabited that planet [Earth], which was the origin of all the men that now occupied the far-flung star systems of the Galaxy."[24]

The book set on Mercury includes the Three Laws of Robotics, with a personal echo for Asimov of "Runaround," the story in which he had first introduced that part of his future. The book set on the moons of Saturn discusses a "language amalgam" that might serve throughout the Galaxy as expansion continues.[25] In all of the six books, continual reminders can be found as to where mankind is headed in the Galaxy—long after David Starr, Bigman, and the Council of Science have become lost and forgotten parts of the origins. So I believe that the emphases of Elkins and Aldiss are wrong. Asimov writing in the Forties and the Fifties may be a bit too much of a cheerleader for the technology of the United States and, even, for "Empire." But his scheme of progress salted with nostalgia does hold together, if not as historical materialism, at least as a vision of generation founded on a lost Golden Age located in our own near future on Earth. He adds new depth, in this way, to the old saw about science fiction as a literature of youth.

NOTES

1. Charles Elkins, "Isaac Asimov's 'Foundation' Novels: Historical Materialism Distorted into Cyclical Psycho-History," *Science-Fiction Studies*, Second Series, ed. R.D. Mullen and Darko Suvin (Boston: Gregg Press, 1978): 138-48. The essay was

originally published in the March 1976 *SFS*. It also appears in slightly longer form in the collection of essays published by Taplinger in 1977, cited earlier in this book. The quotation is from the "Introduction" to the Gregg Press volume written by another *SFS* editor, Marc Angenot, p. xii.

2. Elkins, 144. I find the analysis by Elkins of utopian ideology and Marxist thought particularly good. There is, of course, a whole segment of science fiction study that takes the ideology in the literature as its core. In this book, however, I look more for the unity in Asimov's work. If he does possess ideological unity, it is, I think, the more general Enlightenment ideology of a Godwin, which is looser and more literary than any of the practical ideologies that have come out of the Enlightenment. Such literary anachronism is undoubtedly part of the objection Elkins holds.

3. See in particular the introductory chapter above.

4. See James Gunn's *Isaac Asimov: The Foundations of Science Fiction* (New York: Oxford UP,1982) and Isaac Asimov's *The Alternate Asimovs* (Garden City, NY: Doubleday,1986). Gunn tells the story of the rejection well, p. 141 ff; Asimov tells the same story and silently corrects his misquote.

5. See Algis Budrys, "Books," essay review of *The Early Asimov* and other Asimov titles, *The Magazine of Fantasy & Science Fiction*, June 1986: 18-25.

6. Gregory Benford, "Suffering Fools, Not Gladly," *Science Fiction Review*, Summer 1986: 28-29.

7. Gunn, 143.

8. Asimov, *Pebble in the Sky* (New York: Bantam,1964): 19-20. The book was first published by Doubleday in 1950.

9. See *The Alternate Asimovs* and the shorter version of the story. In a way, the "academic research" that Asimov does fictionally about origins is more important in these stories than are the plots.

10. Gunn, 149. For Asimov's dissatisfactions with the novel and with Horace Gold's editorial ideas, especially about the U.S. Constitution, see Asimov, *In Memory Yet Green: The Autobiography of Isaac Asimov 1920-1954* (Garden City, NY: Doubleday,1979): 580, 600, 612.

11. Asimov reluctantly agreed to Gold's suggestion, but the Doubleday editors liked it. See note above.

12. Brian W. Aldiss, "What Should an SF Novel Be About?" *Fantasy Review*, April 1986: 6 ff.
13. See the discussion in the previous chapter of Asimov's 1953 essay "Social Science Fiction."
14. Asimov, *The Stars, Like Dust* (New York: Ballantine,1983): 66-67. The book was first published by Doubleday in 1951.
16. Asimov, *The Currents of Space* (New York: Ballantine,1983): 56. The book was first published by Doubleday in 1952. Gunn comments that the planet's name is because Asimov is thinking about Liberia, p. 158.
17. David Clayton, "What Makes Hard Science Fiction 'Hard'?" in *Hard Science Fiction*, ed. George E. Slusser and Eric S. Rabkin (Carbondale: Southern Illinois UP,1986): 58-69. Gunn is also good on Heinlein in the introductory material to his anthology *The Road to Science Fiction #3* (New York: Mentor, 1979.)
18. Gunn, *Isaac Asimov. . .* , is good on Asimov regularly turning out these juveniles in the Fifties. He would have titled the seventh *Lucky Starr and the Snows of Pluto* if he had not, as Gunn says, run out of steam with the sixth.
19. *Ibid*.
20. The Yeats' poem is certainly not a work of juvenile literature even though it deals with the poet as an old man visiting a school of young people as a school inspector. Asimov himself is indeed didactic in the reams of science popularization he has written, often for young audiences.
21. Samuelson is particularly good on the literary skill of Asimov in *The Caves of Steel*, which I will take up in the next chapter. See Samuelson, *Visions of Tomorrow* (New York: Arno,1975).
22. See the second chapter above, which deals with Asimov's short fiction.
23. Asimov, *Lucky Starr and the Oceans of Venus* (NewYork: Ballantine, 1984): 33-34. This book was first published by Doubleday in1954.
24. Asimov, *Lucky Starr and the Pirates of the Asteroids* (New York: Ballantine,1984): 152. This book was first published by Doubleday in 1953.
25. Asimov, *Lucky Starr and the Rings of Saturn* (New York: Ballantine, 1984): 156. This book was first published by Doubleday in 1958.

V. ROBOT NOVELS AND TWO NON-SERIES NOVELS

During the Fifties, Asimov was also busy with other fictions. In fact, he himself has identified this period as the Golden Age of his fiction-writing productivity. The notion of peak periods, or Golden Ages, is an elusive notion in science fiction (in Asimov's future history, in his own symbolic anthologizing, and in the periodization of the genre itself). It is appropriate here to notice Asimov's evaluation of his own progress:

> ...most people associate me with the 1940s and think of the positronic robot stories, the Foundation series, and, of course, "Nightfall," as the stories of my peak period. I think they're all wrong. I think my peak period came later—in 1953 and the years immediately following.[1]

A look at the bibliography of Asimov's science fiction will show that the works he refers to are the later juveniles, some of the short stories, but more importantly the robot novels entitled *The Caves of Steel* and *The Naked Sun* as well as the non-series novel entitled *The End of Eternity*. Also, his fine independent novel from the early Seventies entitled *The Gods Themselves* will be treated in this chapter. These works require no apology or special pleading about how they may fit into his overall scheme of future history, though not be successful in their own right as fictions. Unlike one or two of the Galactic Empire novels, each of these works is a superb accomplishment. Further, the latter two novels, even though not part of the future history of Galactic civilization, do develop themes and images that fit Asimov's overall scheme of thought about variability, identity, and change in the nature of things.

When David N. Samuelson wrote one of the early comprehensive analyses of *The Caves of Steel,* which still is one of the best readings of the novel, he opens with the strange assertion that Asimov could not produce such a well-written probe into human character of the future until he had "suppressed his fascination with the Galactic Empire."[2] What Samuelson is getting at is that the specifics of the New York City setting, three thousand years in the future, and of the changing character of the detective hero Elijah Baley in his interactions with his robot partner R. Daneel Olivaw constitute very different literary effects from the broad and sublime images of Trantor, psychohistory, or the spatio-analysts, such as Crazy Rik in *The Currents of Space.* The accomplishment of Asimov, in this first robot novel, is to narrow the window and to zero in on details of character and setting. It would be a mistake to assume that these details are not consistent with and part of the large scheme, that the Godwinian forces of the invisible hand are not also the exact forces which ultimately serve as context for a Lije Baley or a Daneel.

In fact, what Baley must learn, as will be seen and as Samuelson points out, and what the robots continue to "simulate" (on into Asimov's latest novels on the same scheme) is that sharing better communications and changing through the process of communication is the defining characteristic of civilization—whether that civilization is the smaller window of future New York or the larger Galactic window. In other words, insofar as any life can change (and Asimov does believe in understanding and accepting change), it must be a change in "character" and in the relation of character to the environment, such as the machine environment of robots. Thus, for Asimov's overall scheme of thought to make sense (and this is separate from his need to produce entertaining and marketable fictions though it, obviously, has complemented nicely with that need), he must get down eventually to details of character challenged by profound change and to more details in robotics related to character. He does this well in *The Caves of Steel* and in its sequel, and is still working at the images in his most recent sequels.

In a sense, language is the crux in changing human character, just as machine languages drive micro computer robots. It is not change limited just to semantics, however, or to what new words will come into usage. Rather the key is open-ended communication theory, another of the Enlightenment ideals. On the practical language of communication that goes beyond semantics, Samuelson writes well:

> ...man and machine or man and man cannot solve significant problems without communication, especially between opposing viewpoints, which are essentially different frameworks for looking at things. And communication is a key concept in this book [*The Caves of Steel* (Samuelson does not write about the sequel but the same emphasis prevails)], as in much science fiction. Within the fiction, obviously, communication is responsible for breaking down prejudices between characters and between opposing factions. But on the level of technique, also, the book is designed for direct communication from the author to his readers, communication of the gospel of science to the non-scientist, communi-

cation to the scientist of the need to consider humanity. The plots, the mode of presentation, the structure, the level of diction, and the character of the hero—all are directed toward this goal.³

Galaxy editor Horace Gold, who had serialized and made strange suggestions about *The Stars, Like Dust* and who was as James Gunn says "at least as good with ideas as Campbell," suggested originally to Asimov that he write a robot novel that was also a murder mystery. Gold knew how much Asimov was a fan of detective fiction, and the suggestion was ideal, for Asimov later prided himself on mixing the two genres in a "perfect fusion."⁴ Many critics have observed that Asimov's most frequently used and successful plot structure involves the solving of a mystery. In terms of character, as well as language, the challenge of problem solving and of systematically reconstructing a crime that could be interpreted in a variety of ways (the old truism about how different observers see the same facts differently) provides ideal resonance. The character of Lije Baley must, therefore, be one of open-ended curiosity, so much so that even his deeply inbred agoraphobia must be open to some modification during the course of this story and its perfectly symmetrical sequel. If that curiosity were not present, no crime would be solved.

Before describing the wonderfully balanced images of the domed City, as opposed to open space, and the lightening of Baley's agoraphobia as he learns and grows, the basic trait of curiosity and its relation to the practical communication notations that Samuelson stresses above should be made clear. Not only is Baley an experienced police investigator, he is also an amateur historian who is continually curious about the roots of the domed City in over-population, about the medievalist nostalgia for the old Earth among his family and friends, and even about the seemingly alien technological advances of the Spacers with their robots. In other words, like Asimov and many other science-fiction writers, Baley has an open curiosity for all forms of variety, though he himself lives firmly fixed in a particularly neurotic future, replete with details and images that constitute the major effect of the novel and its sequel. As Asimov himself fears flying but fictionalizes flights across the Galaxy, so Baley's character balances his setting with his imagination.[5]

Samuelson sums up one implication of this key character trait well and then identifies it as a "basic human quality distinguishing man from machine":

> Lije's "idle" curiosity is essential in his professional capacity, since a detective never knows what random piece of information may prove meaningful in combination with others.[6]

I think the important notion is randomness or "openness." Detectives, communicators, Godwinians, in fact, must believe in hunch and be open to all sorts of variety and possibility. With the character of Baley and the detail of the two murder mysteries, Asimov has found the perfect vehicle to illustrate the open workings of the invisible hand of the future. For Asimov, rather than total control, such an invisible hand is the only way to conceive of forces such as psychohistory or, much closer to home, the lucky twists and turns of his own career.

Robot Daneel's efficient recognition and yet appropriate machinelike rejection of Baley's open and loose curiosity is representative of a limitation from which the technologically advanced Spacers also suffer. He replies to Baley, "Aimless extension of knowledge, however, which is what I think you really mean by the term 'curiosity', is merely inefficiency. I am designed to avoid inefficiency."[7] Thus, in the human/machine epistemology that these narratives allow Asimov to develop and that is also balanced so nicely along the lines of old and new, or Gold and Iron, a consistent paradox can be detected. Even though the Spacers of the fifty Outer Worlds with their "iron" robots do ultimately bring about the delivery of Old Earth from its womblike reliance on the past and static closeness, it is the human "random" capability for curiosity associated with the "gold" Medievalists rather than machine efficiency that is needed. The Spacers themselves acknowledge this use of the past for working toward the Galactic future.

The murder plots of both novels are symmetrical to each other and at least as paradoxical as the epistemology. In *The Caves of Steel*, the culprit had to get the blaster weapon past the neurotically tight security of Spacertown or had to carry it across open space, which would be impossible for any agoraphobic Earthman. Similarly puzzling is that, even though a robot could have managed the open spaces, a robot could never violate the First Law and murder a man. In *The Naked Sun*, the logical blocks, due to the conditions of neurosis and law, are reversed. The murderer has easy access and freedom of movement. However, no Spacer on Solaria, the underpopulated and open Outer World where Baley bravely has to go to solve this murder, could tolerate the proximity to another human needed for the bludgeon murder. And no robot, of course, could be programmed to violate the First Law. In both cases, however, the clever use of a robot is the crux to the crime.

Just as the crimes and Baley's logical cracking of the puzzles are symmetrical and involve the interaction of robots and men, so also are the key science-fictional themes of the two novels. Mystery writing for Asimov gives way ultimately to the more open-ended speculation about his large Galactic scheme. Although he structures these books in the classic way, so that neither character nor reader knows the solution to the crime till the end of each book, the revelation of the continually expanding Galactic adventure may be the more impressive story effect. At the start of *The Naked Sun,* Baley the practical detective calms his agoraphobia during an airplane flight with a short story from his world about Galactic expansion. He finds it silly reading:

> It was pandering to childishness, this pretense that Earthmen could invade space. Galactic exploration! The Galaxy was closed to Earthmen. It was pre-empted by the Spacers, whose ancestors had been Earthmen centuries before. . . . . They had penned in Earth and their Earthman cousins. And Earth's City civilization completed the task, imprisoning Earthmen within the Cities by a wall of fear of open spaces. . . .[8]

In the course of the two stories, however, Baley changes. He learns that "science-fictional" ideas, such as those in that story, are not silly. He learns that Spacers are, in fact, trying to open up the perspective of Earthmen.

Most significant in Asimov's arsenal of paradoxes in these books is that the Spacers also realize that, in spite of their more advanced technology giving them longer, more leisurely lives (in fact, because of such surfeit), it must be the traits of the Earthmen and their past of "random searching" that have to be utilized. Asimov's understanding of this paradox is penetrating and very important for all his thought about the relation of the past to the present. It is the robot partner who articulates it:

> We crystallized the romantic impulses on Earth into Medievalism and induced an organization in them. After all, it is the Medievalist who wishes to break the cake of custom, not the City officials who have most to gain from preserving the *status quo*. . . . The Medievalist will eventually turn away from Earth.[9]

The realization of Daneel and of the Spacermen, also, is that this process of awakening on Earth, which they have wanted, has begun inadvertently.

To focus on these symmetrically balanced settings and on these details for his Galactic vision, Asimov coins a new concept or image in these books and then uses it well to explore the ironies mentioned above. The image is written in the shorthand of chemistry: "C/Fe," pronounced "see fee," and always written with the diagonal line as it "symbolizes neither one nor the other, but rather a mixture of the two, without priority."[10] Not to be too "alchemical" about Asimov's clear contrast of carbon-based life to the "life" of machines, the resonances here to Golden Age/Iron Age paradoxes are worth emphasizing once again.

Solaria, the Spacer world on which technology has grown to be the most advanced and the most neurotic, is also a kind of Edenic paradise suggesting that "Fe" or fee technology may lead back to the leisure and peace of an Age of Gold. However, on Solaria, such peace is decadent and effete so that Spacers themselves realize that, to be more practical, they need the Old Earth. Not only do the Spacer's request Baley's help but also they clearly see that Medievalist "golden" curiosity is the only way now to advance more space colonization.

Also, the irony of the womb images in both novels is wonderful. The Cities of Old Earth are safe "wombs" and thus, in a way, Golden Ages in themselves. Of course, it is the painful progress out of the womb that humanity needs. The Fetal Farm descriptions and discussions, which help to establish the setting of the technological paradise on Solaria, also suggest the rapid speedup of the ontogeny/phylogeny relationships. Thus the rebirth of Baley's adventuresomeness at the conclusion of *The Naked Sun* has particular promise. The pain and nakedness of birth is one more balance of the old and the new that, in Asimov's future history, is the road to Galactic civilization. The narrator says it very simply about Baley, but the resonance has been established and growth will surely continue: "He had gone out to solve a murder and something had happened to him."[11]

Asimov's detail in these two robot novels about the fifty Outer Worlds originating from Earth is much more profound than in any of his previous fictions about this development outward, and he will return to this vision in his most recent sequels. Also, Gladia Delmarre, the wife of the murdered man in *The Naked Sun* and the prime suspect, represents the introduction of something unusual in Asimov's stories on which both he and James Gunn pause to comment—physical or sexual attraction.[12] In neurotic Solarian fashion, it is only the touch of hands between Baley and Gladia, but the reader will see more of Gladia in her developing sexuality in the sequels, examined in the next chapter. Actually, the complex and important novel *The End of Eternity* (1955), written a year before the character of Gladia, is what Samuelson calls Asimov's closest approximation to a conventional love story. Even here, the depiction of love is never as explicit as the time paradoxes and the heroic assumptions about freedom or determinism. Although the Good Doctor often plays the role of the sexual gallant and did so also in the Fifties, his first love in writing is with the speculation over ideas and general systems.[13]

Significantly, *The End of Eternity* had its own origins in Asimov's character of amateur historian and nostalgia buff. Golden Age yearnings seem deeply ingrained in his personality as well as in his texts. Again, the lucky accident of having something rejected, and then recasting the manuscript, came into play in the making of this book, which he values as one of his best and one the critics have not fully appreciated. (The role of inadvertent "invisible hand," as in the rational Spacers realizing how their intentions are being achieved, is also a major theme in this novel.) In *The Alternate Asimovs*, he prints the original novelette and repeats the account of nostagically thumbing through old volumes of *Time* magazine once he discovered that, as a faculty member at Boston University, he could check out bound periodicals. An advertisement drawing that looked to Asimov, on first glance, like a nuclear-bomb mushroom cloud—in an issue published years before Hiroshima—

started him thinking of time-travel paradoxes, and so he decided to try his hand for the first time at this classic science-fiction motif. The result was immediately rejected by Gold, and rather than try to sell it to Campbell in the short version, Asimov got a contract from Doubleday for an expansion into a novel and completed it by the end of 1954.[14]

Unlike the robot novels or the juveniles that come from this same period and that focus on particular details in the overall scheme of Galactic civilization, *The End of Eternity* (with the wonderful pun in the title) created for Asimov considerations of the most theoretic nature, of purposes or "ends." Ultimately, these lead to a tie-in to and a context for his familiar Galactic scheme. However, the story itself seems to stand alone as an intricate speculation about time-travel and about the invisible hand. Perhaps Asimov needed to back off from imagining Galactic expansion or robotics for a thorough-going examination of the most general bases at the root of his thought, and the lucky revision gave him the opportunity to do this most thoroughly. Also, with the revision, he added the link to his Galactic adventures. He writes:

> I wanted to tie it in somehow with earlier books of mine dealing with the rise and fall of the Galactic Empire. (It's a weakness of mine to try to make my science fiction novels consistent with each other, and it influences my writing to this very day.)[15]

The ideas in the novel wrestle with not only the possibility for the existence of a universe in which adventuresome and "random" Galactic expansion can take place but also with the basic dilemma of how much rational control can be expected to apply in any large system. How specific can the Seldon Plan be? How effectual can rational, long-lived Spacers be? How much of Asimov's own productivity as a writer can he control, or how much time ought he spend browsing through old periodicals? Finally, he opts for a bit of the invisible hand in a Godwinian system that can never be totally rationalized, and it may be within the images, characters, and turns in plot in this most theoretic and yet vivid novel that Asimov works out best his peculiarly irrational sort of rationality.[16]

The plot turns on the classic sort of time paradox: it seems impossible to move back in time and change events so radically that the possibility for the original action is removed. Asimov's setting for the story, however, already involves the total management of such paradoxes by a highly organized bureaucracy. The organization called simply "Eternity" (its members are *not* immortal) has been created following the discovery in the 24th century of the Temporal Field. The purpose of the organization is to adjust events in all centuries and to exert total rational control by sending its workers upwhen or downwhen as needed for "the greatest good of the greatest number." The rational hero the reader knows best from this organization is Senior Computer Laban Twissell. He and his colleagues are dedicated and fascinatingly thorough at the job of total control, and there seems to be much pathos in such dedication: "I have heard (began Twissell) that I was born old, that I cut my teeth on a Micro-Computaplex, that I keep my hand computer in a special pocket of my pajamas when I sleep. . . ."[17]

In one of Asimov's more intricate complications of plot, Twissell and Eternity are defeated, more or less, by circumstance and by other members of the organization who acknowledge forces opposed to total control. However, Twissell and Eternity are tempting as a total network of benevolent management; Asimov makes that clear. Yet, one of the highly trained and skilled subordinates, Andrew Harlan (who in the novel version is the point of view charcter but whose roles had been divided in the early version) comes to question Eternity's control for two reasons. He is led into a love affair by a mysterious Miss Lambent, and he discovers that the invention of the Temporal Field that allows Eternity to exist is dependent on a time paradox. The inventor used equations that were not derived till three centuries later. Eternity knows about this accidental, non-rational wrinkle and is working to rationalize it. Twissell insists in both versions that no paradoxes exist.

To find a safe place and time for his mysterious love (she seems to drive it all as, perhaps, a sort of pale, invisible hand), Harlan decides to send the individual he has been told to use to correct the time paradox far back, beyond the 24th century, into the primitive era. Under pressure from his bosses and since he is good at primitive history (it's his hobby, as it was Baley's), Harlan locates the lost traveler in the 32nd year of the 20th century (1932 or 19.32), trying to convey a message through a *Time* advertiscment similar to the one Asimov had seen. Harlan goes to 1932 with Lambent and learns from her then that she is actually from the Hidden Centuries. Eternity had known about this strange period of 80,000 years way upwhen that had been closed to their workers for some reason. Lambent explains to Harlan that, in this future, humanity advances to even more control of time and space than Eternity. In fact, the supermen there are so ethereal (so much more like computers) that they are just discovering interstellar space travel (apparently with rational control one does not need to travel much) only to find the Galaxy inhabited by other intelligent races.

Thus the suggestion is that these supermen, working like invisible hands through Lambent, are actually hoping to break up the static utopian effects of Eternity so that humanity can get to the stars sooner. The supermen of the Hidden Centuries had discovered one timeline they call the Basic States, which is *our* timeline of early nuclear power, space flight, and Galactic expansion. The lovers know they would rather have such an open adventure than all the contol of Eternity and inadvertently it happens. It happens, just happens, in 1932 (primitive times) when Asimov himself is twelve years old. So he has established the link to his Galactic schemes, but the more profound link is the invisible hand: "He wasn't even aware that he had made his decision until the grayness suddenly invaded all the sky as [Eternity] disappeared." His lover had just reassured him about his inadvertent decision: "Eternity will go and the Reality of my Century, but *we* will remain to have children and grandchildren, and mankind will remain to reach the stars."[18] In the early version, Asimov had not destroyed Eternity; in the revision and expansion, he found his roots.

If Asimov's roots are in open-ended possibilities and in large, general schemes of history and origins, the coming decade of the Sixties and his award-winning novel of the early Seventies, *The Gods Themselves,* were a real test of confidence and direction for him as writer of science fiction. Gunn implies that "getting to the stars" for Asimov, associated with the realities of Sputnik and our own space program, meant turning in his own career to the writing of non-fiction, especially on science. Gunn also points out how clearly Asimov realized that science fiction itself was the hardest sort of writing for him.[19] Also, his autobiographical recollections seem to make it clear that when the New Wave writers, such as Roger Zelazny and Harlan Ellison and the British, were the strongest in the sixties, Asimov feared that his own large fictional schemes were outmoded. Some of his expressions of this fear, in fact, suggest how deeply rooted was his sense of passing time and of lost Gold or lost Titanism: "Now it was I who was one of the dinosaurs, and there was a New Wave of mammals, whom I scarcely knew and who wrote in ways I could scarcely understand."[20]

Although he produced little science fiction during this decade, his energy and enthusiasm as writer and producer of books never waned. He expresses great glee over all the deals connected with *Fantastic Voyage* (1966), his movie novelization that saw first serial publication not in any of the science-fiction magazines but in *The Saturday Evening Post*. As Gunn argues, the exhilaration of real space expansion is important to Asimov.

Asimov writes:

> On February 3, 1966, the Soviets made the first soft landing on the Moon and obtained photographs of its surface *from* its surface. These were the first surface photographs. . . . I felt exhilarated enough to tackle the last bit of *The Universe* [a book of science popularization].[21]

A minor character working for Eternity near the beginning of that novel, however, had made a contrast between literature and real science in a way that has never left Asimov. This comment may serve as a motto for bridging these dry years that he now has recovered from so well: "I hope you'll forgive me for using picturesque language rather than precise mathematical expressions."[22] *The Gods Themselves* (1972) not only is one of the richest "picturesque" fictions Asimov has written, strong in images, but also it is much more successful with sensual details of writing, even sex, and with a sublime science-fictional core of speculation—than any New Wave fan might have expected from the Good Doctor. If the new writing produced a crisis of confidence in Asimov, he recovered well with *The Gods Themselves*. Further, as in his fictions, the fear of losing track forever with Golden origins has now become moot, I think, since his autobiographical outpourings and subsequent understandings of recent years, as well as his Galactic expansion sequels that are still coming, seem to be producing no static rest in this remarkable career of Golden Ages.

Nevertheless, when he wrote *The Gods Themselves*, he knew it was a revival for him of strong science-fiction writing and of strong image creation. He even was afraid momentarily (or more correctly his future wife Janet was) that he might not live to put the final, polishing touches on the work when a trip was coming up to interrupt the writing.[23] Also, like so much in his career, the origin of the story had an inadvertent, accidental base that he acknowledges and seems to analyze fully in his autobiographical recollections. The fuller account is in *In Joy Still Felt;* in *The Alternate Asimovs* he chooses not to identify Robert Silverberg as the one who first amused him by the notion of plutonium-186 but correctly associates the book with *The End of Eter-*

nity as a short piece that grew, under pressures of its own images and publishing needs, to become a novel.[24]

The images themselves are what drive the story. After Asimov had worked out a plausible and detailed storyline to explain the impossibly unstable plutonium isotope that Silverberg's slip of the tongue had given him and after he had built images for how indirectly science and scientists often work and how alien messages might be interpreted by a skilled linguist, he was asked to expand more. So he turned to the parallel universe where plutonium-186 was a natural element and then returned in a third section to more sociology of accident and "stupidity" in the most rational of human activities—science—and finally to more cosmic speculation about other parallel universes and about the equilibrium that might be established among universes in which sub-atomic forces balance one another.

Not only would this cosmology that Asimov creates in the book involve delicate balances in the electron population to avoid either anemic drains or explosive destruction of whole universes, but also the book itself is a *tour de force* of symmetrical organization. In three arenas, he demonstrates the truth of his title motto from Friedrich Schiller: "Against stupidity, the gods themselves contend in vain." His account of the vagaries of scientific work in the near future is as seemingly accurate as anything in fiction till Gregory Benford's recent novel *Timescape,* which surely used both this work and *The End of Eternity* as models. The three sections of the book are mirrored in the Triad alien creatures of the middle secton, and the midpoint of our universe, between the para-universe and the Cosmeg universe (echoes of the Cosmic Egg image from 18th-century cosmology as suggested in the introductory chapter to this book with the mention of Carl Sagan), also suggests continually adjusting symmetries. A comment near the conclusion of the book evokes the symmetry of the Seldon Plan, but again it is only Asimov's mode of thought and not any specific link to his Galactic works: "In any case, there are no happy endings in history, only crisis points that pass."[25]

From his autobiographical account, however, as well as from the interest that the critics have shown, Asimov wrote best in this novel when he imaged the aliens of the middle section. These images are rich with suggestions not only about sexuality (which Asimov nearly chortles with glee over in in his autobiography—to have pulled off so well) but also about the relation of the sensual to the intellectual, about life after death, and about threepart combinations of identity and personality that range from Freudian to Christian overtones.[26] This is hard science-fiction extrapolation at its best because the aliens seem plausible in their own amoebic, energy-starved reality and also suggestive to the reader of what it seems like to be human. The following passage may be read as sensual, Trinitarian, religious in our terms, and at the same time as clearly decipherable in alien terms. The "male" speaker is telling his "female" partner about how he sees now "through a glass darkly, then face to face":

> Listen, Dua, whenever we melt, whenever the triad melts, we become a Hard One. The Hard One is three-in-one, which is why he is hard. During the time of unconsciousness in melting we are a Hard One. But it is only temporary, and we can never remember the period afterward. . . .there comes the possibility of the

final stage, where the Rational's mind by itself, without the other two, can remember those flashes of Hard One existence. Then, and only then, he can guide a perfect melt that will form the Hard One forever, so that the triad can live a new and unified life of learning and intellect. I told you that passing on was like being born again. I was groping then for something I did not quite understand, but now I know.[27]

Thus with a poetic art of "the word," unusual for him, Asimov leaves this image of the alien trinity of individuals planted suggestively for readers. It is a fine accomplishment. Fortunately, it was not his last. When he returns to science-fiction novels, he returns to his large scheme—his more characteristic and open-ended poetry.

NOTES

1. Isaac Asimov, *In Memory Yet Green: The Autobiography of Isaac Asimov 1920-1954* (Garden City, NY: Doubleday,1979): 680. His 1974 anthology *Before the Golden Age* was the initial catalyst for my interpretation of "Golden Ages" in his work.
2. David N. Samuelson, *Visions of Tomorrow* (New York: Arno,1975): 124. The study was a doctoral dissertation completed in 1968, one of the early ones on modern science fiction.
3. *Ibid.*, 150-51.
4. James Gunn, *Isaac Asimov: The Foundations of Science Fiction* (New York: Oxford UP,1982): 109-110. See my previous chapter for more on Gold and Asimov in the early Fifties.
5. Alan Elms, a member of the psychology department at the University of California at Davis and a colleague in the Science Fiction Research Association, is currently engaged in research on Asimov's own agoraphobia.

6. Samuelson,149.
7. Asimov, *The Caves of Steel* (New York: Ballantine,1983): 192. This book was first published by Doubleday in 1954.
8. Asimov, *The Naked Sun* (New York: Ballantine,1983: 3. This book was first published by Doubleday in 1957.
9. *The Caves...*,189.
10. *Ibid.,* 50.
11. *The Naked...*, 207.
12. Gunn, in particular, is delighted to have been sent a letter by Asimov, when he was working on the hand-touching scene between Gladia and Baley, joking about his use of sensuality, 130.
13. See chapter 55 in the first volume of the Autobiography, cited above, for a candid statement by Asimov about sexuality and about its relation to his energy and confidence in writing. The comment by Samuelson is in his entry on Asimov in *Twentieth-Century Science Fiction Writers*, ed. Curtis C. Smith (New York: St. Martin's,1981): 28.
14. See Asimov, *The Alternate Asimovs* (Garden City, NY: Doubleday,1986) for his partiality to this book.
15. *Ibid.,* 210.
16. See, in particular, my discussions earlier on Godwin in chapter three and on rationality in chapter one.
17. Asimov, *The End of Eternity* (New York: Fawcett,1971):148. This book was first published by Doubleday in 1955. In the short version, Asimov says less delicately of Twissell: "It was also said that at an early age his heart had atrophied and that a hand computer similar to the model he carried always in his trouser pocket had taken its place." (*The Alternate Asimovs*, 156). Despite, or indeed because of, the ironic treatment, Twissell's drive for control is still tempting to Asimov, in my reading.
18. *The End of...*, 191.
19. Gunn, 189.
20. Asimov, *In Joy Still Felt: The Autobiography of Isaac Asimov 1954-1978* (Garden City, NY: Doubleday,1980): 418.
21. *Ibid.,* 389.
22. *The End of...*, 12.
23. *In Joy Still Felt...*, 575.
24. *Ibid.,* 552. Also, see *The Alternate Asimovs*.

25. Asimov, *The Gods Themselves* (New York: Fawcett1973): 287. This book was first published by Doubleday in 1972.
26. *In Joy Still Felt. . . .* , 567.
27. *The Gods. . .* ,165-66. For a set of images treating metamorphosis of symbiotic alien life forms into a sort of immortality, see the fine Hal Clement novel, *Cycle of Fire* (1957).

VI. LATE NOVELS AT THE CUTTING EDGE

A fine history-of-science study, published in 1960, carries a title that continues to evoke both the clever power of language and the nature of Enlightened thought itself. *The Edge of Objectivity,* by Charles Coulston Gillispie, refers to both the latest pioneering efforts of science and the "cutting edge" of analysis.[1] When Asimov, as a young man, arranged to have Hari Seldon's Foundation set on Terminus, a planet at the "edge" of our spiral galaxy, and the Second Foundation hidden on Trantor at "Star's End," which was actually near the center (he corrects that location now knowing that a Black Hole may be the center) or at the other end of the spiral, he was evoking the same set of rich double meanings in the tiny words "end" and "edge." So it is very characteristic that the next Foundation book, *Foundation's Edge* (1982), should toy even further with this image by locating these ends or edges not only in space but also in time.

Asimov's historical scholar or "scowler" in this book, Janov Pelorat, who is a Foundation man, even though the pun on scholar comes from Asimov's depiction of Second Foundation academics here, suggests these punning possibilities to the hero Golan Trevize:

> . . .in Gaal Dornick's account of the day of the trial before the Imperial court. "The other end of the Galaxy"—those were the words Seldon had used to Dornick [Asimov quoting himself] and ever since that day their significance had been debated. . . . [what] connected one end of the Galaxy with "the other end"? Was it a straight line, a spiral, a circle. . . . It was perfectly

clear that the one end of the Galaxy was Terminus. It was at the edge of the Galaxy, yes—*our* Foundation's edge—which gave the word "end" a literal meaning. It was, however, also the newest world of the galaxy at the time Seldon was speaking, a world that was about to be founded. . . . What would be the other end of the Galaxy, in that light? The other Foundation's edge? Why, the *oldest* world of the Galaxy? And according to the argument Pelorat had presented—without knowing what he was presenting—that could only be Earth.[2]

In this way Asimov remarkably resumes and, in fact, deepens his theme of the quest for origins. When this award-winning sequel is over and the story of the Seldon Plan, intended to minimize the effects of the Fall of the Galactic Empire, extended farthest forward in time to the end of the 5th century of the Foundation Era (or roughly half way through Seldon's promised thousand years), no one of the factions, which now include both Foundations as well as the gestalt of the telepathic and mysterious new planet Gaia, has yet spiraled back to discover the origins on Earth. Asimov will work to close that loop in his most recent sequel, *Foundation and Earth* (1986).[3] At least that less-punning title promises to move the action forward in time to deal with more of the Seldon Plan.

In the meantime, his two other late novels, *The Robots of Dawn* (1983) and *Robots and Empire* (1985), continue to fill in details and link the parts of his future history about Galactic expansion out of Earth with the role of robotics, "humanics," and psychohistory in this expansion. Further, all four of these novels from the middle years of the decade of the Eighties (an age in Asimov's life when most men as successful as he are retiring) are firmly at the "cutting edge" of Asimov's ideas and are wonderful novels of ideas.

The ideas continue to resonate from the Enlightenment—Golden Age images about origins and analyses of, as well as puzzlements over, control through "laws," such as robotics or psychohistory. Underlying all this are assumptions and beliefs about the invisible hand of determinism or "what is intended to be," associated with Godwinian Necessity . Certainly Asimov's energy and hard work as he himself grows older is driven by a "necessary" compulsion that he has something important to say. Twissell's circular reasoning on his certainty about being on the right track for Eternity from Asimov's most intricate novel with Godwinian ideas, *The End of Eternity,* which contains the same telltale pun in its title as noted above, reveals much about Asimov's own confidence that as long as his energy holds out he must be doing the right thing:

> To give the 20th [century] information we know they did not have would be as damaging to [Eternity's schemes] as would wrong action on our part. We're still here, so in his [the agent they sent back] whole lifetime in the current Reality of the Primitive he's done no harm of that sort.[4]

Though this view is proved wrong at the end of the story in favor of random openness, I think a part of Asimov himself is driven Twissell-like by the belief that he can and must close up loose ends in his thought. The novels of the Eighties, even though inevitable loose ends still remain, are remarkable for their comprehensive, consistent, and interesting Asimovian concepts.

Age and its repeated expressions have not dulled the edges for Asimov of his sublime notions about historical development and about the puzzle of the role of the individual and of humanity in such inevitability. In fact, these four late books of his long fiction dance a kind of minuet of chiasmus around the major themes and two "kinds" of novel in two series that Asimov had alternated between in his early career. Never to imply that the work of such a strong writer is complete while he is still "here," nevertheless, the symmetry and sense of recapitulation in this late work contains a remarkable balance and sense of movement toward closure. Both the 1982 and 1986 novels are Foundation stories that push the destiny of humanity in the Galaxy farthest forward in time and that raise the most penetrating questions about origins and the causes of things. In these books with these topics, Asimov's large, ambitious ideas make him seem like a modern Lucretius. (He started in on Roman history with Campbell and is himself, in his own non-fiction writing, an historian so such comparisons, though facile, may not be inappropriate.)[5] Sandwiched between these two extensions of the Foundation series are two novels that carry on the series of Robot novels. The pattern of publication is reverse parallelism, or chiasmus, which was a favorite Enlightenment pattern. The Robot novels are less sweeping in their movement, closer to novels of character. Gladia the Spacer heroine, Baley from the Caves of Earth, and humanoid robots who nearly achieve human characters are the images that people these stories as they also provide more details leading toward Empire, psychohistory, and beyond. If Asimov resembles Lucretius, scientist and natural historian, as he reaches toward a coherent cosmology, he is like Vergil, poet of the *Aeneid,* as he points toward the founding of Empire as well as the sadness when great founders must die before the promised land is reached.

The weaving back and forth among these four late novels of the threads of a vast story that he began to tell more than four decades earlier is surely a *tour de force* for Asimov. Close reading will no doubt discover flaws and inconsistencies. What is not inconsistent is the overall pattern, not only the shape and ambition of the four books read together but also the overall effect of a set of grand themes. Perhaps these are even politically important for modern man, as the Romans cited above intended their work to be important for the continuation of Rome. Asimov has become more of a "strong poet" with age. As this chapter will show, his sort of poetry is more that of the large, epic design and puzzlement over the cosmos than the smaller and suggestive images of character in *The Gods Themselves.* These four late novels reaffirm Asimov's strongest fictional effect.

Rather than just "gee whiz" wonder at expansion into space or sentimental nostalgia over lost youth, both of which are simpler effects for which Asimov in the typical science-fiction tradition might have settled, paradox and the continual deepening and complication of the big themes mark each of these late fictions. It seems to be the philosophic puzzle of causation and purpose that drives these books—and that may have driven Asimov back to fiction. There is, in fact, nearly a surfeit of images to express this puzzle. One big word for the notion is "orthogenesis." Though Asimov does not burden the stories with the word itself, every turn of image, plot, and characterization is haunted by the question of the nature of purposeful evolution.[6] In *Foundation's Edge,* the gestalt-planet Gaia, which will grow to the organically unified and gestalt-galaxy called Galaxia, represents the ordained and general "law." However, the decision, or choice, to move Galactic expansion in that direction is given to one individual human, Trevize. The final novel, then, will puzzle over how the hero *knew* to follow the correct hunch and to make the right decision. No law could tell him to follow the law. In other words, decision or choice may be grounded more on hunch and on individuality than on law and generality.

In the Robot novels, the puzzle emerges again in the differences between Spacers and Earthmen as well as in the extent and nature of robot control. Asimov wrings out an addition to the Three Laws: the Zeroth Law is used to abstract the purposeful direction of humanity in general. He has telepathic robots designed by Spacer technology derive this Fourth Law. He links such benevolent despotism to psychohistory and ultimately to the total control of Gaia and Galaxia. Still he retains the need for individual human choice, not to mention that someone had to make the machines who derive the laws. Long before Golan Trevize's role as the hero who makes a choice, the hero robots Daneel and Giskard puzzle over the question of how direction and "newness" can ever be inserted into a system of Law:

> "You gave a perfect answer, friend Giskard...
> "It was the best answer within the compass of the Three Laws. It was not the best answer possible."

"What was the best answer possible?"

"I do not know, since I cannot put it into words or even concepts as long as I am bound by the Laws."

"There is nothing beyond the Laws," said Daneel.[7]

The problem, then, is the question of from where, eventually, the Fourth Law comes. A related problem is that if Law is done away with, allowing for random "newness," nothing in the way of historical development can be sure. Reading Asimov brings to mind such questions.

Asimov's title for this third late novel, *Robots and Empire*, is nearly as evocative as his use of the word "edge" in the title of the 1982 opener to the set. Not only do the words refer to the two series of his that are brought together in these books but also the images represent the deep paradox in his thought. There were no robots, of course, that figured prominently in the original *Foundation Trilogy* or in the Galactic Empire novels. Similarly, in the Robot novels, Spacer technology, which had the skill to create humanoid machines as excellent as Daneel and Giskard, seemed to lack the daring and adventuresomeness to settle the Galaxy. The paradox is clear. Robots themselves must transcend their own creators and make plans *secretly* for the expansion of humanity into the rest of the Galaxy. Thus rather than robot or human expansion, which had been the apparent contrast earlier, the synthesis is robots and Empire, or a thoroughgoing C/Fe symbiosis. But the questions still remain—both of origins and of individual choice.

The related notion is the paradox of Godwinian philosophic anarchy and the invisible hand of control. A foreshadowing, which becomes deepened in the opening pages of *Foundation's Edge*, is the secret and mentalist control exerted by the Second Foundation—as well as the Robotics Institute of the Spacer worlds in the next two books. It was Godwin's son-in-law Percy Shelley who referred to poets as the "unacknowledged legislators of mankind," and the image for political management that Asimov seems to prefer is that intellect prevails over raw power. Even the Mule represented this balance. The "smartest" roboticist, Fastolfe, will lead the Institute, in a parody of this principle, and the Second Foundation "scowlers" are memorable and tough politicians.[8]

Asimov's deepening of the puzzles in the continual quest for origins, also, is impressive in these late books. Whereas the Foundation stories and the Galactic Empire novels contained mysteries over the location of the Second Foundation as well as scholarly speculation about Earth as seedbed of all future evolution, Asimov's serious accumulation of argument in these most recent novels broadens well what he began in his first published novel. *Pebble in the Sky*, the first novel, contained Bel Arvardan's seminal dissertation on origins. The books of the Eighties go much further into near-academic research questions about origins. The reasoning often sounds like linguistic speculation over the Ur language linguists today call Indo-European. The theory is that it was in use once because of consistency in derivations that still exist. Asimov works the same theme through speculations based on the existence in his future of Galactic Standard Time—"GSD" for Galactic Standard Day. No planet familiar to Pelorat, or Trevize, has exactly the time periods that are Galactic Standard. Thus there must have been one common ancestor.

Further, in all four books and with increasing frequency, language analysis and even the analysis of fragmentary inscriptions figure in the search for Earth or in the later encounters between Spacers and Earthmen in *Robots and Empire,* just before the radioactive planet is "forgotten" as the site of all origin. The impression is that the late Asimov has become somewhat more linguistically sophisticated as a speculator on origins than the young fan of Roman history or the beginning novelist of *Pebble in the Sky*. A stone inscription in the fourth novel carries a reversed letter F, and the name Gaia echoes earliest Greek myth, millennia before either Asimov himself or the Roman Empire. Strangely, though, the rather blunt word "Spacer" is left entirely alone by Asimov and survives unchanged in all the stories. He is writing adventure and science fiction, finally, and not linguistics.

Nevertheless, insofar as these late novels are scholarly games, they encourage the reader to draw on what is known about such things as fragments of Greek in the study of Bible texts and inscriptions all over the ancient world and then to project more than two hundred centuries into the future when Earth itself, carrying all the history that is now known as history, has been lost and forgotten. The method is, also (as always with Asimov) wide open and general so that his characters doing their searches must reason by analogy because what is most interesting to them cannot be known except by analogy. When he returns in the fourth novel especially, Trevize, who becomes the Lije Baley of the 20th millennia after Earth's disappearance, continually asks the question: "Is this a true analogy?"[9]

Though clearly the suggestion is thus made to the reader to maintain a running comparison with historical patterns that fade back into Early Church history and into ancient Greek and Roman history, Asimov's own future history finally is made more or less complete in these four novels. The total future time frame is somewhat more than 23,200 Galactic Standard years or Earth years. Baley and Robot Daneel flourish three thousand years in the future. Gladia Delmarre, the Spacer, has lived another two centuries by the time of *Robots and Empire*. Then the lapse is 20,000 years until the Foundationers, Trevize and Pelorat, go in search of the lost Earth and also find Gaia. In the meantime, what takes place is that after Daneel and Robot Giskard derive the Zeroth Law of Robotics, which allows the interests of all humanity to be taken into consideration under "law" and after the poignant deaths of both Giskard and Baley, narrated in *Robots and Empire*—Daneel himself creates Gaia, plans for Galaxia, and has his servant robots systematically lift all records of Earth and hence records what is programmed for the good of humanity in the Galaxy.

I will return to this major theme of total programming for the general good, as it is tied in so well by Asimov to the notion of origins. Before this, however, the sketch of the overall plot fulfillment in these four related novels needs to be made complete. By the time of the middle of the Seldon Plan, not only Earth but also the fifty original Spacer worlds all seem to have disappeared. Thus Trevize—along with the Asimovian, curious historian Pelorat, the Gaian beauty Bliss, and a strange alien child they find on Solaria—must sail a future Odyssey from one lost Spacer world to another till they eventually rediscover Earth where, wonder of wonders, they find Daneel still functioning but moved to the Moon. Operating on the Seroth Law, Daneel has determined that the Seldon Plan and Second Foundation mentalics ought to be replaced by the more total control and unity of Gaia and eventually Galaxia. Daneel feels he has need of individual, human choice, however, to make the decision for unity. That is where Trevize's thorny intellectual puzzle in *Foundation and Earth* enters the picture.

Another way to look at this overall scheme, which shows Asimov wonderfully linking together his Foundation stories and his Robot novels, is to focus on each of the four late books in turn, with the shape of chiasmus in mind as mentioned above. *Foundation's Edge* creates the first view of Gaia and the hoped-for Galaxia, moves the Second Foundation puzzles to the back of the story, and resumes the theme of origins from *Pebble in the Sky* and from the Galactic Empire novels. The team of the hero and his intellectual companion, a sort of Holmes and Dr. Watson relationship, is nicely established. The novel concludes with the surprising individual choice that will dominate the latest sequel.

In *The Robots of Dawn,* Asimov brings Lije Baley, who by the end of these sequels Asimov has almost enshrined as the legendary culture hero of the Galaxy, and Daneel firmly back into his work. He speculates in this novel far beyond the limits on sexuality and machine intelligence that prevail in the earlier Robot novels. In fact, to a greater extent in this late novel than in the others, he seems to speculate at the edge of conventions, even at the edge of taboos. Though he is not as great a taboo-breaker, obviously, as other science-fiction writers such as Theodore Sturgeon and Harlan Ellison, Asimov engages here in as much ratiocination about taboos as any of them. He speculates about sex, about sex between man and machine, about isolation and toilet habits, and about the relation of robotics to "humanics" in anticipation of the Zeroth Law and the ultimate programming that will be the puzzle later on in the sequels. However, in this rather thick novel, in particular, he seems to want his reader to believe that he will talk cogently and theoretically on any topic. Such liberation of the topics for speculation, though the times have changed too, may be the newest element in Asimov's work of the Eighties.

For example, here is a discussion of "Personals," or toilets, in the over-crowded world of the Spacers. It is remarkable how much the characters go in and out of toilets in this novel. In the following passage, Baley speculates about the strange behavior of someone actually speaking to him in the toilet:

> How strange it was, thought Baley, that he was so pleased to get out from behind walls and into the Outside. There was something more totally alien to this Personal than anything else he had encountered on either Aurora or Solaria. Even more disconcerting than the fact of planet-wide indiscriminate use had been the horror of being openly and casually addressed—of behavior that drew no distinction between this place and its purpose and any other place and its purpose.[10]

As usual, Asimov toys with the possibilities at a high level of generality and joins, here, his running speculation about closed versus open spaces to the speculation about privacy in toilets. Moreover, he does not push for conclusions about anality or any other Freudian constructs or to fix on any of the nightmare fantasies that can come from analysis that is *not* left open. Rather, the writing seems to vibrate with the notion that inevitable and complex analysis will not only allow speculation to reach anywhere (even into toilets) but also assure some linkage to the hope for overall rational system.

In *Robots and Empire*, then, with the more liberated Gladia still alive because of Spacer technology and working now with a descendant of the legendary Baley to promote the more adventuresome, non-Spacer expansion into the Galaxy that will lead to Empire and beyond, Asimov flashes back to capture the important last rendezvous between Lije and Gladia. Just as overt sexuality is mentioned more freely in Asimov's late fiction, so too Lije and Gladia progress from the touch of hands to full sexuality, at least by implication. Also, this book contains the death scene of Baley, with Daneel there—a fine C/Fe scene—and then Giskard's poignant "death." Further, Giskard and Daneel derive the Zeroth law in this book and set the tone for resuming with Godwinian speculation, that is, a speculation more focused on cosmology and origins. (Sexuality and toilets were also interesting to Godwin and "sublime" for 18th-century thinkers as for Asimov.) However, origins and cosmology were where Trevize had left off in the first of these late books.

Finally, *Foundation and Earth* picks up with Trevize's determination both to understand why he made the choice of Gaian unity (and why it was necessary to have an individual choice for a system that subsumes the individual) and to find the lost Earth. Trevize is completely liberated sexually though Asimov still writes more vividly on puzzles of determinism and individual freedom than on this topic. The structure of the story is a somewhat monotonous jumping from planet to planet till they eventually find the Earth that Spacer bitterness had centuries before made radioacative, its haven Moon, and Daneel. Asimov does leave an opening suggestion at the end of the novel for alien forces from outside our Galaxy (he will produce more novels), but essentially he has completed his story of how humanity and machines made by humanity will unify the Galaxy for the good of all people.

The Godwinian notion of unified and "necessary" control, as opposed to a robust and random individuality, is the key intellectual puzzle that Asimov works through again in this most recent of his novels. Rather he resolves the contrast as a genuine paradox. Trevize, as one individual, must decide to make the right choice to institute the Gaian planet-organism that will eventually lead to the super-organism of Galaxia. At the end, it is revealed that Daneel, who as the brilliant machine that he is, conceived and implemented the unity and control of Gaia, actually sought out the proper individual to serve as "hero" who would make the proper choice so that the choice can, in fact, be a freely elected "Necessity." The circle goes round and round and is a genuine paradox as, to make the choice a genuine choice and more credible, Trevize agonizes over it throughout the book. He learns gradually that complete individuality, or the characters they call "Isolates," as represented best perhaps by the excessively neurotic Solarians who escape into "caves," acts as a sort of malignant withdrawal from the Galaxy. Just as the womblike Caves of Steel prevented expansion in the

Galaxy over 20,000 years before, so neurotic individuality is a threat to the future Galaxy. Bliss is correct when she says to Trevize, "If a human-inhabited world breaks up completely, is truly Isolate, and if it loses all interaction with other human worlds, it develops—malignantly." At the same time, Trevize is suspicious of too much control. He is a strong individual, and the proper balance is always in question in his mind:

> I don't say the old Galactic Empire was ideal, and I can certainly see flaws in the Foundation Confederation, but I'm not prepared to say that because total Isolation is bad, total Unification is good. The extremes may each be equally horrible. . . .[11]

Ultimately, he does choose Gaia, the move toward total unification. Still, he is always puzzled why he made that choice.

More than space adventure or sexual adventure, it is this intellectual probing of the possible balances between the individual and the large system that saturates *Foundation and Earth* as well as the three novels that come just before—with, perhaps, the exception of *The Robots of Dawn*. Asimov seems most comfortable with such a large, general theme and with one that will always remain a paradox partly because one can never cease discussions of it and partly because neither the randomness of individuality nor the certitude of a perfect machine is acceptable by itself. Humanity may never uncover the final origin, but one of the ultimate puzzles is exactly this question of who or what makes anyone choose the right choice and how can it be a choice if anyone is *made* to choose it in the first place.

The point is made early in the story that only human beings, rather than their machines, have this gift of reaching correct conclusions on the basis of incomplete data. Human origins may be the only key to the mystery. Though Asimov has future Earth rediscovered, the mystery still remains. Calvin, Godwin, Asimov, and many others wrestle with this mystery and may wrestle far into the night.

NOTES

1. As an historian and a scientist himself, Asimov is no doubt familiar with Gillispie's study that was first published by Princeton UP.
2. Isaac Asimov, *Foundation's Edge* (Garden City, NY: Doubleday,1982): 94-95.
3. The further development of his future history in this most recent novel is no longer a matter of guesswork.
4. Asimov, *The End of Eternity* (New York: Fawcett,1971): 158. This book was first published by Doubleday in 1955.
5. He even makes use of a Latin quotation in the third sequel of these late novels. Asimov, *Robots and Empire* (Garden City, NY: Doubleday,1985): 216.
6. For this Enlightenment notion, see my paper "The Discovery of the Future and Indeterminacy in William Hazlitt," *The Wordsworth Circle* 8:1 (Winter 1977): 75-79.
7. Asimov, *Robots and Empire*, 22.
8. P.B. Shelley's "Defence of Poetry" was first published in 1821.
9. Asimov, *Foundation and Earth:* 135.
10. Asimov, *The Robots of Dawn* (Garden City, NY: Doubleday,1983): 245. My ideas about speculation in this novel are developed more fully in a paper written for the annual meeting of the Science Fiction Research Association in 1984.
11. Asimov, *Foundation and Earth* (bound page proofs): two quotations, part of one dialogue on pages 258-59.

VII. CONCLUSION

Neither Asimov's fictional time schemes for future Galactic history nor his laws governing the interactions of machines and humans are as accurate as the scientist in him might demand. One of his most harsh critics of late, who has reviewed with some scorn even the recent sequels, has stated clearly in another context and in lay terms why it is not plausible to accept the science of Galactic expansion:

> . . .there was much talk of "the galactic community," and some discussion of a "United Nations of the Stars," but the absurdity of this was quickly appreciated. Interstellar distances are too great to sustain any meaningful communications, let alone communities. It is now widely accepted that there will be no union between the star-worlds, whether inhabited by "humans" or "aliens." There can be no galactic empire, or federation. . . .[1]

But even the terminology of this judgment, in which Brian Stableford and David Langford are not specifically writing about Asimov, attests to the solid accomplishment of the Good Doctor as fiction writer and visionary. Asimov's peopled galaxy and his puzzles over technological order, as opposed to human freedom, have become part of the thinking of our time. In his fictions, though scientific plausibility on the small level of individual details is always maintained, his visions for a coherent history and for human possibilities are of the utmost importance. In other words, social science fiction, as Asimov terms it, takes precedence over gadgetry for him. Further, he adds his own intensity and remarkably energetic voice to these large, conventional visions that were part of the genre long before he began to write. However, the critics who object to the facileness and optimism of science fiction, again have Asimov at the point to draw their fire. This, in itself, is part of his accomplishment. He has come to stand for the visions of the genre he first began to love in his father's candy store.

The literary style and polish of this vision, also, is open to attack. Asimov tends to repeat ideas too much since they are so fascinating to him, and thus he depends too often on long and didactic sections of dialogue that read like teaching sessions. Paradoxically for a writer so interested in humanity, characters may serve primarily in some stories as mouthpieces for ideas, and the robots themselves, especially in *Robots and Empire*, may be given the more interesting ideas to become even the more interesting characters. David Samuelson and James Gunn, who are the most sympathetic and perceptive commentators on Asimov's fiction, agree that his writing style best fits his matter in the more character-focused and lean Robot novels of the Fifties.[2] Although I agree, I would add that Asimov's skill in articulating profound intellectual puzzles in clear and intense prose, notwithstanding narrative repeats, is the more characteristic and valuable hallmark of his work. He achieves this puzzle depiction best in *The End of Eternity* and in the final four novels to date.

One can be certain that Asimov has no intention of stopping. Along with the late sequels, he has also produced recently several juvenile novels in collaboration with his wife, Janet Jeppson. The project entitled *Fantastic Voyage II*, his own narrative sequel to the novelization of the film he did in the Sixties, has also appeared.³ There is always the central vision of humanity and machines in our Galaxy with alien life just beyond, as he alludes to at the end of *Foundation and Earth*. So, though I have attempted to highlight provocative themes from this monumental body of fiction, this book cannot hope to be an exhaustive study. No one knows what plots and what ideas are yet to be described. I would hope that these pages may work as a guide to the seriousness of Asimov's ideas as well as the human focus of his vision.

Finally, balanced against these solemn, grand notions is always the wise sense of proportion that is comic in Asimov's work. I cannot argue this fully here though I have attempted to do so elsewhere, but this comic awareness is characteristic of much of the more important hard science fiction. Here is a telling comment that a perceptive shipmate inserts about Asimov's latest hero, Golan Trevize:

> "You do have this annoying habit of trying to turn everything into a joke, but I know you are under tension and I'll make allowance for that."⁴

The tension that Asimov himself feels is not only from his ambition as a writer, which has been always very strong, but also from his sense of the vastness of things. Science-fiction writers may be able to perceive this vastness more clearly than other writers. Thus, when Asimov peoples the Galaxy or resolves the man/machine symbiosis or speaks to the most enigmatic questions of origin and freedom, it is all, in a sense, hopeful thinking punctuated with a nervous laugh. One result has been this important body of fiction that in its totality and depth is no joke but rather a genuine gift.

NOTES

1. Brian Stableford and David Langford, *The Third Millennium, A History of the World: AD 2000-3000* (New York: Knopf,1985): 210. Stableford is the one who has written harsh reviews of the recent novels.
2. Samuelson and Gunn have been cited in previous chapters and appear in the Secondary Bibliography. Gunn has continued to comment and in particular has produced two fine essays on the late sequels that were published after his Oxford UP study. These also appear in the Secondary Bibliography and were helpful in my chapter on the late sequels.
3. This fine new story, which I was able to read while making corrections in this manuscript, further illustrates both the personal focus in the fiction of Asimov and his effort to wrestle with godlike issues. Beginning by pointing out that the sequel is entirely his own work rather than having been written from a screenplay that others did, Asimov proceeds to construct a lively fiction of a voyage on a miniature vessel into a human brain. This story has its strongest effect, perhaps, in the intellectual chess of rationality that is so characteristic of his work. For Asimov, also, the story represents both a return to the Soviet Union and a fascination with deep psychoanalytic notions, but grounded in the "reality" of physics.
4. Isaac Asimov, *Foundation and Earth* (Garden City, NY: Doubleday, 1986): 234. My longer study *Comic Tones in Science Fiction* is cited in chapter one above and is listed in the Secondary Bibliography.

VIII. SELECTIVELY ANNOTATED PRIMARY BIBLIOGRAPHY

This is a selected list in three categories: science-fiction novels, science-fiction short-story collections, and autobiographical writings in book-length form. Within each category only the original publication of books is listed, and the order of listing is chronological. Many of the novels, as well as most of the shorter forms, had first publication in magazines. Also, in this book, I have often cited from later reprints as well as from short nonfiction pieces by Asimov in magazines, and for each of these citations full bibliographic information appears in the notes. Complete bibliographies of such a prolific writer as Asimov are books in themselves. The Miller volume listed in my Secondary Bibliography below is excellent. Also, the checklist at the end of the Gunn volume, listed below, is fine and lists items, privately printed and rare, that I have not seen.

Science Fiction Novels

Pebble in the Sky. Garden City, NY: Doubleday,1950. In this Galactic Empire novel, Earth is already dangerously radioactive and the "scholarship" about origins begins.

I, Robot. New York: Gnome,1950. Unified around the character of Susan Calvin, these stories make one story, and the Three Laws of Robotics are introduced.

The Stars, Like Dust. Garden City, NY: Doubleday,1951. More on Earth origins in this least successful of the Galactic Empire novels.

Foundation. New York: Gnome,1951. The Seldon Plan of psychohistory is first introduced to bring order to the chaos at the end of the Empire.

David Starr: Space Ranger. Garden City, NY: Doubleday,1952. The first juvenile. Asimov uses the name Paul French for this and the other Starr books. This one is set on Mars.

Foundation and Empire. New York: Gnome,1952. This continuation of the Seldon Plan stories introduces an individual, the Mule, who disrupts order.

The Currents of Space. Garden City, NY: Doubleday,1952. The third Galactic Empire novel; Earth as origin remains uncertain and nice metaphysical speculations are included.

Second Foundation. New York: Gnome,1953. The end of the Trilogy, in which second Foundationers are finally discovered on Trantor itself.

Lucky Starr and the Pirates of the Asteroids. Garden City, NY: Doubleday, 1953. More science for juveniles about the Solar System and humanity expanding into space and, ultimately, the Galaxy.

The Caves of Steel. Garden City, NY: Doubleday,1954. Introduces detective Baley and Robot Daneel and the continuing conflict between Earthmen and Spacers over the expansion into space.

Lucky Starr and the Oceans of Venus. Garden City, NY: Doubleday,1954. The third Paul French juvenile, same themes.

The End of Eternity. Garden City, NY: Doubleday,1955. Perhaps his most complex speculation on order and freedom, it sets a context for Galactic expansion.

Lucky Starr and the Big Sun of Mercury. Garden City, NY: Doubleday,1956. Robots and robotics are more actively involved in this juvenile with echoes back to *I, Robot*.

The Naked Sun. Garden City, NY: Doubleday,1957. Baley and Daneel solve a murder on Solaria, the youngest Spacer world, and meet Gladia.

Lucky Starr and the Moons of Jupiter. Garden City, NY: Doubleday,1957. Wonderful panoramic view of the Solar System and robotics again.

Lucky Starr and the Rings of Saturn. Garden City, NY: Doubleday,1958. The last of these juvenile novels. When he returns to juvenile novels in collaboration with his wife, it is different.

Fantastic Voyage. Boston: Houghton Mifflin,1966. Novelization of a film. Asimov wrote neither the script nor the original story, though the novel came out before the film.

The Gods Themselves. Garden City, NY: Doubleday,1972. Story of symmetrically balanced universes and his most wonderful aliens, triad creatures.

Foundation's Edge. Garden City, NY: Doubleday,1982. Halfway into the Seldon Plan, Foundationers go looking for a Second Foundation trick and for Earth and find Gaia.

The Robots of Dawn. Garden City, NY: Doubleday,1983. Baley goes to solve a crime on the oldest Spacer world, Aurora, and becomes more involved with Gladia.

Robots and Empire. Garden City: Doubleday,1985. Gladia, two centuries older but still trim, teams up with a Baley descendant and with robots to ensure Earth's expansion into the Galaxy, though Earth is left growing radioactive at the conclusion.

The Norby Chronicles. New York: Ace,1986. This is a bringing together of two juvenile stories written in collaboration with his wife, Janet Jeppson. Thus this is not the first book publication for this, and they had also done two other Norby juveniles, which I have not seen.

Foundation and Earth. Garden City, NY: Doubleday, page proofs scheduled for publication October 1986 and uncorrected. (Since I used the proofs due to the generosity of the publisher, I list the book in this way; it did appear on schedule.) Setting out from Gaia, the Foundationers finally rediscover Earth and find Daneel still functioning to maintain order.

Fantastic Voyage II: Destination Brain. Garden City, NY: Doubleday,1987. In order to unlock secrets of the brain, five voyagers enter the brain of a Soviet scientist who is in a coma.

Science Fiction Short Story Collections

The Martian Way and Other Stories. Garden City, NY: Doubleday, 1955. Includes "The Martian Way," "Youth," "The Deep," and "Sucker Bait."

Earth Is Room Enough. Garden City, NY: Doubleday, 1957. Includes "Satisfaction Guaranteed," "The Fun They Had," "Kid Stuff," "The Immortal Bard," "The Last Trump," "Franchise," "Dreaming Is a Private Thing," "The Message," "The Dead Past," "Hell-Fire," "Living Space," "Someday," "The Watery Place," "Gimmicks Three," and "Jokester."

Nine Tomorrows. Garden City, NY: Doubleday, 1959. Includes "Profession," "The Feeling of Power," "The Dying Night," "I'm in Marsport without Hilda," "The Gentle Vultures," "All the Troubles in the World," "Spell My Name with an S," "The Last Question," and "The Ugly Little Boy."

The Rest of the Robots. Garden City, NY: Doubleday, 1964. Includes "Robot AL-76 Goes Astray," "Victory Unintentional," "Satisfaction Guaranteed," "Risk," "First Law," "Let's Get Together," "Galley Slave," and "Lenny."

Nightfall and Other Stories. Garden City, NY: Doubleday, 1969. Includes "Nightfall," "Green Patches," "Hostess," "Breeds There a Man. . .?," "C-Chute," "In a Good Cause—," "What If—," "Sally," "Flies," "Nobody Here But—," "It's Such a Beautiful Day," "Strikebreaker," "Insert Knob A in Hole B," "The Up-to-Date Sorcerer," "Unto the Fourth Generation," "What Is This Thing Called Love?," "The Machine That Won the War," "My Son, the Physicist," "Eyes Do More Than See," and "Segregationist."

The Early Asimov. Garden City, NY: Doubleday, 1972. I considered including this book in the next category of autobiographical writings because the commentary between the stories is so important. The collection includes 27 early stories. The most important are "The Callistan Menace," "Trends," "Black Friar of the Flame," "Homo Sol," "The Imaginary," "History," "Death Sentence," "Blind Alley," "The Red Queen's Race," and "Mother Earth."

The Best of Isaac Asimov. London: Sphere, 1973. Stories here in first book publication are "Marooned Off Vesta" [this had appeared in *Asimov's Mysteries* from Doubleday in 1968], "Anniversary," "The Billiard Ball," and "Mirror Image."

Buy Jupiter and Other Stories. Garden City, NY: Doubleday, 1975. Asimov's running commentary on the stories is in full swing by this collection that includes 24 rather unimportant new stories. Most interesting are the title story and "Thiotimoline to the Stars."

The Bicentennial Man and Other Stories. Garden City, NY: Doubleday, 1976. The most interesting of these 12 new stories is the title story, and it is a more sentimental departure for robotics. Asimov's long fiction seems more central by this point in his career.

The Winds of Change and Other Stories. Garden City, NY: Doubleday, 1983. Again the running commentary is as interesting as the stories, but the appearance of a version of the early story "Belief" in conjunction with *The Alternate Asimovs,* listed in the next category, is important here, as are the two new stories—"The Last Answer" and "The Last Shuttle." In all, there are 21 stories here.

The Edge of Tomorrow. New York: Tor, 1985. A mixed collection in which he includes with non-fiction some of his favorite stories. It is significant that he prints here the later draft of "Belief," revised to please Campbell, then within a few months prints the earlier draft in *The Alternate Asimovs,* listed below in the next section.

The Best Science Fiction of Isaac Asimov. Garden City, NY: Doubleday, 1986. Collection of 28 short pieces, some verse, chosen by himself with usual biographical commentary. Most date from the decade of the Fifties, so he might have titled it "The Middle Asimov."

Robot Dreams. New York: Berkley, 1986. Includes a story "Lest We Remember," not yet collected.

Autobiographical Writings

The Hugo Winners. Garden City, NY: Doubleday, 1962. In the commentary he wrote for this anthology, Asimov begins the persona and the autobiographical thrust that will become so apparent in his writing.

Before the Golden Age. Garden City, NY: Doubleday, 1974. This wonderfully nostalgic collection of science fiction stories that Asimov loved as a teenager carries on the autobiographical mode very effectively.

In Memory Yet Green. Garden City: NY: Doubleday, 1979. The first volume of his massive autobiography that takes the story up to 1954.

In Joy Still Felt. Garden City, NY: Doubleday, 1980. The second volume of the autobiography.

The Alternate Asimovs. Garden City, NY: Doubleday, 1986. Early versions of "Belief," *Pebble in the Sky,* and *The End of Eternity,* along with recollections and commentary. The textual problems for future scholars studying Asimov ought to be interesting, and he seems to try to arrange for this himself. He publishes within months of this book, in a different publication, another version of "Belief." See entry in the previous section of this bibliography for *The Edge of Tomorrow*.

IX. SELECTIVELY ANNOTATED SECONDARY BIBLIOGRAPHY

Though certainly not as booming an industry as the commentary on the work of Ursula K. Le Guin, for example, Asimov criticism has grown steadily over the years until any sensible critic entering the discussion must be selective in the citation of predecessors. The list below contains what I have found most valuable in this study, as well as references to materials dealing with ideas from the 18th-century Enlightenment that also support my reading of Asimov. I exclude listing here some short reviews for which bibliographic information may be found in the notes.

Aldiss, Brian. "What Should an SF Novel Be About?" *Fantasy Review* 90 (April 1986): 6 ff. Raises important questions about Galactic Empire images in Asimov and others.

Allen, L. David. *Asimov's Foundation Trilogy and Other Works*. Lincoln: Cliff's Notes, 1977. Some value on fictional technique.

Bloom, Harold. "Freud, the Greatest Modern Writer" *New York Times* 23 March 1986, Book Review Section: 1, 26-27. Clear and direct statment of the importance of Freud.

Boyd, John D. *The Function of Mimesis and Its Decline*. Cambridge: Harvard UP, 1968. Good on the methodology of the Enlightenment.

Brigg, Peter. *Reader's Guide to J.G. Ballard*. Mercer Island, WA: Starmont, 1985. Helpful in describing the antipathy of the more "literary" science-fiction writers to Asimov, Campbell, and their colleagues.

Budrys, Algis. "Books," essay review of *The Early Asimov* and other Asimov titles, *Fantasy & Science Fiction* 421 (June 1986): 18-25. Like many of Budry's long reviews, this contains important literary criticism.

Chapdelaine, Perry A., Sr., Tony Chapdelaine, and George Hay, eds. *The John W. Campbell Letters. Volume I*. Franklin, TN: AC Projects, 1985. Later volumes should have more letters from Campbell to Asimov.

Cioffi, Frank. *Formula Fiction? An Anatomy of American Science Fiction, 1930-1940*. Westport: Greenwood, 1982. Good on the differences between science fiction and other writing.

Clayton, David. "What Makes Hard Science Fiction 'Hard'?" in *Hard Science Fiction*. Ed. George E. Slusser and Eric S. Rabkin. Carbondale: Southern Illinois UP, 1986: 58-69. Interesting psychoanalytic reading, of which we need more.

Culler, Jonathan. *On Deconstruction*. Ithaca, NY: Cornell UP, 1982. Helpful on intertextuality.

Doody, Margaret Anne. "Insects, Vermin, and Horses: *Gulliver's Travels* and Virgil's *Georgics*" in *Augustan Studies*. Eds. Douglas Lane Patey and Timothy Keegan. Newark: U of Delaware P: 145-74. The Georgic is a favorite 18-century effect.

Elkins, Charles. "Isaac Asimov's 'Foundation' Novels: Historical Materialism Distored into Cyclical Psycho-History" in *Science-Fiction Studies*. Second series. Eds.

R.D. Mullen and Darko Suvin. Boston: Gregg, 1978: 138-48. This important essay was originally in the March 1976, issue of *SFS* and also appears in the Olander and Greenberg collection of essays listed below.

Fiedler, Jean, and Jim Mele. *Isaac Asimov*. New York: Ungar, 1982. The least useful of the books on Asimov—stresses his short fiction.

Goble, Neil. *Asimov Analyzed*. Baltimore: Mirage, 1972. Analyzes style with word counts and treats both fiction and non-fiction.

Godwin, William. *Enquiry Concerning Political Justice and Its Influence on Morals and Happiness* (1793) selections in *Backgrounds of Romanticism*. Ed. Leonard M. Trawick. Bloomington: Indiana UP, 1967. Trawick's editing is very useful, as are his notes, for understanding this key Enlightenment thinker.

Gunn, James. *Isaac Asimov: The Foundations of Science Fiction*. New York: Oxford UP, 1982. The best study to date; Gunn has overcome the limitation of his early publication date to some extent with two discussions of the sequel novels as listed immediately below.

_____. "Polishing the Robots." *Fantasy Review* 69 (July 1984): 9-11.

_____. "Son of Foundation." *Fantasy Newsletter* 58 (April 1983): 15-17. Both discussions are in the same journal (that underwent a change in title).

Hardesty, William H., III. "The Gods Themselves." In *Survey of Science Fiction Literature*. Ed. Frank N. Magill. Englewood Cliff, NJ: Salem, 1979: 909-913. A fine, short study.

Hassler, Donald M. "Autobiography and Science Fiction: Children of Rousseau and Wonder." *Extrapolation* 26 (1985): 277-84.

——————. *Comic Tones in Science Fiction*. Westport, CT: Greenwood, 1982. This book contains reprints of my essays on "Golden Age" ideas in Asimov and on Hazlitt and the "future"—the first appeared originally in the Olander and Greenberg collection listed below.

——————. *Erasmus Darwin*. New York: Twayne, 1974.

——————. *Reader's Guide to Hal Clement*. Mercer Island, WA: Starmont, 1982.

Happenheimer, T.A. "Man Makes Man." In *Robotics*. Ed. Marvin Minsky. Garden City, NY: Doubleday, 1985. 49-51. One entry to the vast literature on robotics that mentions Asimov.

Miller, Marjorie M. *Isaac Asimov: A Checklist of Works Published in the United States, March 1939-May 1972*. Kent: Kent State UP, 1972..

Moskowitz, Sam. *Seekers of Tomorrow: Masters of Modern Science Fiction*. Cleveland: World, 1966. A fine early essay on Asimov.

Olander, Joseph D., and Martin Harry Greenberg, eds. *Isaac Asimov*. New York: Taplinger, 1977. The most important collection of critical essays on Asimov.

Patrouch, Joseph F., Jr. *The Science Fiction of Isaac Asimov*. Garden City, NY: Doubleday, l974. His own first-person "perambulations through Asimov's works," well organized around the forms that Asimov uses.

Pawling, Christopher, ed. *Popular Fiction and Social Change*. New York: St. Martin's, 1984. Good on the notion of paraliterature.

Robinson, Kim Stanley. *The Novels of Philip K. Dick*. Ann Arbor: UMI Research Press, 1984. Along with the Brian Stableford reviews mentioned below, Robinson is the best example of the attempt by the more "literary" SF commentators to dismiss Asimov.

Sagan, Carl. *Contact*. New York: Simon & Schuster, 1985. A most recent extension of the "conventions" that Asimov contributed so greatly to that reading this fiction helps one comprehend Asimov.

Samuelson, David N. *Visions of Tomorrow.* New York: Arno, 1975. The chapter in this book, together with his reference book entry in *Twentieth Century Science Fiction Writers,* edited by Curtis Smith, establish Samuelson as the second most useful commentator on Asimov, coming just after Gunn.

Sante, Luc. "The Temple of Boredom." *Harper's,* October 1985: 66-71. A strong attack.

Stableford, Brian, and David Langford. *The Third Millennium, A History of the World: AD 2000 - 3000.* New York: Knopf, 1985. In this fine book, Asimov is credited with seminal vision; in Stableford's recent reviews of the sequels, he has carped about growing tediousness.

Warrick, Patricia S. *The Cybernetic Imagination in Science Fiction.* Cambridge: MIT Press, 1980. Most useful in describing the move toward robotics that Asimov continues much to in his fiction.

Wollheim, Donald A. *The Universe Makers.* New York: Harper & Row, 1971. Good on future history.

INDEX

Ackerman, Forrest J., 13
Aldiss, Brian 63, 72
Alternate Asimovs, The, 31, 59, 84, 90
"Among School Children" (Yeats), 69
Anderson, Poul, 22
Asimov, Isaac,; see also discussion of specific works
Asimov, Janet (Jeppson), 113
Asimov on Science Fiction, 10
"Azazel" stories, 30, 31

Baley, Elijah, 76, 78-84, 99, 104, 105, 106, 108
Ballard, J.G., 21, 22
Beat poets, 21
Before the Golden Age, 12
"Belief," 25, 32
Benford, Gregory, 60, 91
Best of Asimov, The, 26
Bible, 27, 29, 47, 104
"Bicentennial Man, The," 44
"Black Friar of the Flame," 18
Budrys, Algis, 60
Byron's *Don Juan*, 11

Calvin, John, 38, 39, 41
Calvin, Susan, 37, 38, 39, 41
Campbell, John W., Jr., 5, 14, 18, 20, 21, 22, 23, 32, 44, 85, 99
Caves of Steel, The, 75, 76, 77, 80
Challenger, 30
Clarke, Arthur C., 11, 12, 14, 30
Clayton, David, 68
Clement, Hal, 5, 64
Coleridge, Samuel Taylor, 9, 10
Complete Robot, The, 44
Conklin, Groff, 38
Contact (Sagan), 27
Currents of Space, The, 65, 66

Daneel, see Olivaw
Darell, Arkady, 53
de Camp, L. Sprague, 46
Decline and Fall of the Roman Empire (Gibbon), 46

Delmarre, Gladia, 83, 84, 99, 105, 108
Detective fiction, 4, 29
Dua, 92

Early Asimov, The, 12, 19, 21
Edge of Objectivity, The, (Gillispie), 96
Elkins, Charles, 56-57, 63, 68, 72
Ellison, Harlan, 89, 106
Emerson, Ralph Waldo, 32
Encyclopedia Galactica, 49
End of Eternity, The, 75, 84, 90, 91, 98, 113
Enlightenment, The, 7, 8, 9, 11, 14, 16, 20, 23, 27, 28, 45, 77, 99
"Evitable Conflict, The," 40

Fantastic Voyage, 89
Fantastic Voyage II, 114
Foundation stories, 99
Foundation and Earth, 97, 106, 108, 110, 114
Foundation and Empire, 50
Foundation's Edge, 8, 96, 101, 103, 106
Foundation Trilogy, The, 37, 45, 48, 49, 102
Frankenstein motif, 44
French, Paul (Asimov) 69
Freud, Sigmund, 10
Frost, Robert, 5

Galaxy, 63, 78
Georgic mode, 51
Gibbon, Edward, 46, 47, 50
Giskard, R., 101, 105, 108
Gods, Themselves, The, 75, 88, 90, 100
Godwin, William, 39, 41, 53, 103, 108
Gold, H.L., 14, 63, 64, 78, 85
"Grow Old Along with Me," 59
Gunn, James, 14, 38, 60, 69, 78, 84, 88, 89, 113

Hamilton, Edmund, 21
Harlan, Andrew, 87
Heinlein, Robert A., 21, 57, 68, 69
"Homo Sol," 24

I, Robot, 37, 39, 40, 41, 42, 43, 53
In Joy Still Felt, 90
Isaac Asimov's Science Fiction Magazine, 14, 33

Joyce, James, 21
Juvenile fiction, 69, 113

Knight, Damon, 9

"Last Answer, The," 28
"Last Question, The," 28
"Last Shuttle, The," 29
Lem, Stanislaw, 14
Locke, John, 37
Lone Ranger, The (radio series), 69
Long, Ted, 26, 70
Lucky Starr, 26, 69, 70, 72
Lucretius, 99, 100

"Marooned Off Vesta," 13
"Martian Way, The," 26, 28, 70
McCarthy era, 26
Milton, John, 8, 28, 29
Minsky, Marvin, 15
Mule, The, 51, 52

Naked Sun, The, 75, 80, 81, 83
"Nightfall," 32, 33, 50, 53, 61, 75

Olivaw, R. Daneel, 80, 101, 105, 106, 108, 109
Omni, 42
On the Road (Kerouac), 21
Opus 300, 10

Pebble in the Sky, 22, 58, 59, 65, 103, 104, 106
Pohl, Frederik, 14, 18, 38, 69

Riose, Bel, 50, 51
Robotics, see "Three Laws" and "Zeroth Law"
Robots and Empire, 97, 102, 104, 105, 108, 113
Robots of Dawn, The, 97, 106, 110
Rousseau, Jean-Jacques, 9, 10
"Runaround," 42, 72

Sagan, Carl, 12, 14, 15, 28, 30, 92
Samuelson, David, 70, 76, 78, 84, 113
Saturday Evening Post, The, 89
Schiller, Friederich, 91

Second Foundation, 52, 103
Seldon, Hari, 24, 49, 51, 53, 57, 60, 96, 97
Shelley, Percy, 103
Simak, Clifford, 21
Sky, 33
"Social Science Fiction," 45
Stableford, Brian, 112
Stapledon, Olaf, 28
Starr, David, 26, 70, 72
Stars, Like Dust, The, 63, 64, 71
"Story Behind 'Foundation'", The, 48
"Sturgeon, Theodore, 21, 106
Swift, Jonathan, 6

The 1,000-Year Plan, 48
Three Laws of Robotics, 38, 40, 42, 43, 72
Time, 84, 87
Timescape (Benford), 91
Toynbee, Arnold, 46
"Trends," 20, 21, 27
Trevize, Golan, 96, 101, 104, 105, 108, 110, 114
Twissell, Laban, 86, 87, 98

Vergil, 100
Voltaire, 7, 27, 28, 32

Williamson, Jack, 21
Winds of Change and Other Stories, The, 29
Wright, Thomas, 15

Yeats, William Butler, 69

Zelazny, Roger, 89
Zeroth Law, 101, 105, 107, 108

www.ingramcontent.com/pod-product-compliance
Ingram Content Group UK Ltd.
Pitfield, Milton Keynes, MK11 3LW, UK
UKHW041436180426
11947UKWH00007B/475